*We're Going to the Chapel*

# CONTENTS

# Borders

# THE ULTIMATE
# Quilt Finishing Guide

## Batting, Backing, Binding & 100+ Borders

Harriet Hargrave *and* Carrie Hargrave-Jones

*Fancy Tail Feathers*

C&T PUBLISHING

Text and photography copyright © 2021 by Harriet Hargrave and Caroline Jones

Artwork copyright © 2021 by C&T Publishing, Inc.

Publisher: Amy Barrett-Daffin

Creative Director: Gailen Runge

Acquisitions Editor: Roxane Cerda

Managing Editor: Liz Aneloski

Editorial Compilers: Roxane Cerda

Cover/Book Designer: April Mostek

Production Coordinator: Zinnia Heinzmann

Production Editor: Alice Mace Nakanishi

Production Assistant: Lauren Herberg

Illustrators: Wendy Mathson, Kirstie L. Pettersen, and Aliza Shalit

Photography by Brian Birlauf, unless otherwise noted

Published by C&T Publishing, Inc., P.O. Box 1456, Lafayette, CA 94549

Library of Congress Cataloging-in-Publication Data

Names: Hargrave, Harriet, author. | Hargrave-Jones, Carrie, 1976- author.

Title: The ultimate quilt finishing guide : batting, backing, binding & 100+ borders / Harriet Hargrave and Carrie Hargrave-Jones.

Description: Lafayette, CA : C&T Publishing, 2021.

Identifiers: LCCN 2020040413 | ISBN 9781644031001 (trade paperback) | ISBN 9781644031018 (ebook)

Subjects: LCSH: Quilting. | Stitches (Sewing) | Borders, Ornamental (Decorative arts)

Classification: LCC TT835 .H3386 2021 | DDC 746.46--dc23

LC record available at https://lccn.loc.gov/2020040413

Printed in the USA

10 9 8 7 6 5 4 3 2 1

The authors take full responsibility for the contents of this book, including the technical accuracy of the information. Please direct any questions to quilt.academy.q.a@earthlink.net.

Please visit the Quilter's Academy blog, too, for additional information and discussions: quiltersacademy.blogspot.com.

*Goose in the Pond*, featuring many borders

Photo by C&T Publishing

Adding borders to your quilt top is a wonderful way to frame the design developed by the piecing. The border is a place where you can stop the repeat piecing design and give your eye a place to stop or rest.

A single border is often enough for a simple quilt pattern. A combination of two or more plain strips around the outside edge of the piecing can be more exciting, and adding corner blocks can add another design element.

A border can draw the eye inward and reinforce the design of the overall quilt top, or it can be so busy that it competes with the interior design of the quilt top. There are a couple of approaches to finding out what will work best. One is to totally plan the quilt on paper, including the borders, to see if the scale and the complexity of the border enhance or detract from the quilt top. The design, width, and number of fabrics are determined before cutting and sewing.

If the quilt top is finished, you can audition simple borders at the design wall. You can get a real feeling for the effects of the color, pattern, and placement of different fabrics on the overall look of the quilt. You may find that what looks good on paper does not always play out the same in the actual fabrics.

Determining the width of simple strip borders—either single or multiple—is easier when the quilt top is finished. As you audition different fabrics, you will see how their color and value play a part in how wide they need to be cut. It is hard to predetermine width until the border is next to the edge to which it will be added. You will also find that the fabrics used in the quilt top are not the only choices. Adding a totally new fabric can really pull a design together and add spark.

# Choosing Fabrics for Borders

Borders act as frames around your entire quilt top. These fabrics need to enhance your quilt, not detract from it.

Think about the following ideas when planning your borders:

• Because of their position and purpose, the color of the border fabrics can influence the color scheme of the entire quilt. The color used for the border can be the same color as found in the blocks, or it can introduce a whole new color that enhances the quilt's overall effect. Repeating a predominant color combined with adding one or two new colors can give striking results. Fabrics such as solids and stripes are especially interesting in borders.

• Using a large-scale print that contains the colors of the fabrics in the quilt top can have a dramatic effect and can pull all the colors together, unifying the quilt top, borders, and/or sashings.

• Border stripes create a coordinated look to the overall quilt. With mitered corners, the border becomes an elaborate frame, but with very little effort.

• Consider how you want to quilt the borders. Remember that a busy printed fabric can be your friend by hiding stitching issues, but it will not let the quilting design show. A solid or small-print fabric allows the quilting to be a focal point, but it will not do much to hide any quilting issues you may still be working out. With practice comes excellence, and you may find that challenging yourself to quilt a solid border is a good way to leapfrog your abilities forward.

*Tip* ❋ It is often easier to select border fabrics once all the blocks are made. Take the blocks to your quilt shop and "audition" them with a variety of fabrics. Stand back and study the effect that different colors and different fabrics can give. You will start to see that the fabric you choose to work with can and will affect the width of each border. For fun, ask a total stranger for an opinion. But remember, this is your quilt, and you will make the final decision. If you like what you have picked, go with that; you will be happier and will have a happy quilting experience that way!

# CHECKING THE QUILT TOP
## — FOR SQUARENESS —

*Town Square*

Once your quilt top is completed and well pressed, you need to check that it is square. Are the two sides the same length, and are the top and bottom the same width? Then you'll need to measure the entire quilt top to determine the length needed for the borders. The first step is to fold the quilt top in half to determine whether the top and bottom edges are the same width as the center, and the two sides are the same length. To do this, fold one end of the quilt top over to the center as shown. Are the top edge and center the same width? Repeat with the other end. Do the same with the sides, one side at a time. Are they the same length?

Folding quilt top to center

# Correcting for Deviations

As you pieced your quilt top, you should have squared up each unit as you went along. This process really helps develop a quilt top that is very accurate. If everything is perfectly even, you're ready to measure and cut the border strips. But what if things don't come out even? Perhaps one side is longer than the other, or one end is shorter than the other. Now is the time to make corrections.

Harriet does this by examining the piecing of the seams where the rows are joined. It is a common problem for the fabric to pivot slightly as you're nearing the end of any seam, especially if you are using a zigzag throat plate. If this is happening, then it's possible that a slightly larger or smaller seam was taken at the edge, making that side of the quilt shorter (or longer) or narrower (or wider) than the opposite side, where the seam started. Just one or two threads' width difference per seam can throw off the measurements dramatically. If this is the case, restitch, being careful to keep the needle just beside the previous stitching. If the seams need to be smaller, release the stitches back from the edge about 3″ to 4″, and restitch, being careful to not stitch in the same holes a second time.

> *Hint* ✳ When folding your quilt top in half, line up the seams of corresponding blocks. This often shows which seams or blocks are off. They should line up exactly across from one another.

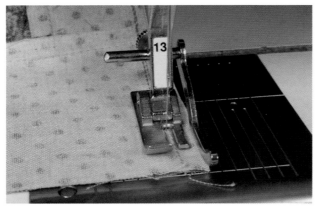

A deeper seam being taken

Whatever you determine, attempt to make corrections until the top is within ⅛″ or less of being even when it is folded in half and measured.

Check for accuracy by folding the edge to the center after each correction. You don't want to overcorrect. Often one correction is enough to fix the problem. In the end, you want both sides to be exactly the same length, and both the top and bottom to be the same width. *Never cut or trim to correct size discrepancies!*

## Using a Ruler to Straighten Edges

Next, use a square ruler 16″ or larger to check all four corners. Are they perfectly square, at perfect 90° angles? When placing a square ruler on the corner, use the straight and diagonal lines of the ruler to align with the inner seams of the blocks.

Everything needs to be aligned with the ruler lines as closely and as parallel as possible. If the corner is not perfectly square, shave away any little bits that are causing the problem. *Remember—do not do this before you check the length and width of each side of the quilt top. You cannot correct an internal piecing problem by whacking off the corner to make the sides and the top and bottom the correct length. This action will only distort the shape and measurements of the units in the corner.*

If the corner is really out of square, look at the internal piecing of the block in the corner. Adjust the seam allowances first as described, and if the corner is not perfectly square, you can then shave off threads to correct this.

This is very important because when the first border is sewn on, the border will continue the out-of-square problem, and the finished quilt will not lie flat or hang straight.

Use a 24″-long ruler and rotary cutter to clean up the side edges of the quilt top. Measure out from any seams to make sure that you are not cutting too deep into the body of the quilt top. Remember, you are just cleaning up the edge of ragged threads. The edge pieces should measure their intended finished dimension plus ¼″. If you cut too deeply, the dimensions of the units within the block along the edge will not stay accurate. For example, if the squares of your four-patch should finish at 2″, but you cut into the side of one or more of these squares, they will not measure 2″ finished and will not appear square when the quilt is finished.

Once the top and bottom edges of the quilt top are even with the center (the same length as the center on both sides), and the corners are square, you're ready to measure for and cut your borders.

# Squaring a Diagonal Set Quilt Top

Squaring up a diagonal set quilt is a bit different from working with a straight set quilt. Diagonal sets present different concerns. Because everything is diagonal (on the bias), the method of measuring for straight set quilts does not work. Instead, you need to work off the points of the blocks that are along the sides of the quilt top. It would be great if you could just measure out from the points and cut off any excess fabric that is not wanted along the edge! Unfortunately, it's not quite that simple.

Once the quilt top is finished and the final pressing is done, it is time to find a large flat surface that will allow you to measure across the width and/or length of the quilt top. You also need to decide how much of the side-setting triangles are going to extend beyond the corners of the blocks; do you want the binding to butt right up against the points, or do you want to float the triangles out beyond the corners?

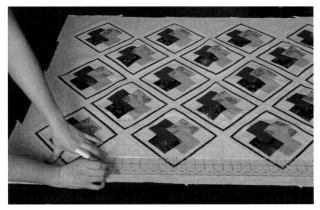
Ending with triangles right at corners of blocks

1. Measure the desired distance from each block corner and make a mark. Do this on all four sides of the quilt top.

Measuring from block corners

2. Measure across the width of the quilt top. You are trying to establish one width measurement that will be consistent down the length of the quilt top. Measure from one mark across the quilt top to the opposite side. Note the measurement. Continue doing this at every mark across the quilt. If all the measurements are the same, it is your lucky day! Unfortunately, that is not generally the case. You will probably see a bit of a difference from one pair of marks to the next. The goal is to establish the same width down the quilt sides by adjusting the marks to be further out or closer in where

needed. The marks will not all be the same distance from the block corners; this is only a problem if you are planning to finish the binding right up to the corners. If you want to float the blocks, this adjustment will be barely noticeable.

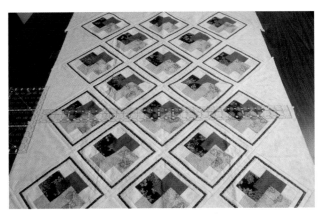

Measuring across the top from mark to mark

3. Repeat Step 2 for the length of the quilt top by measuring from end to end and checking the measurement at each mark. Adjust and re-mark as necessary.

4. Use a long straightedge to join the marks into a straight line. Be sure that the marker you are using will completely come out of the fabric, as you are marking the seamline for a border or for the binding.

Joining the marks for a straight edge

5. Use a large square ruler to square the four corners. Align the ends of the right angle with the lines you just established—say at the top and side of one corner. Once these lines are connected, check within the ruler to make sure that the ruler lines are squared and aligned with the interior piecing of the blocks and setting triangles.

Squaring the corners

6. Once everything is square, draw a line to connect the corner with the sides. Repeat for all four corners. Next, measure out ¼″ and draw another line. This will be the cutting line—*but don't cut the edge yet*. If no borders are going to be added to the edge beyond the setting triangles, you are ready to mark, layer, and quilt the top. Use this excess fabric along the edge as a handle to help you control the edge as you quilt. Once the quilting is finished, the edges can be remeasured and trimmed. Because quilting can cause some contraction and distortion, always remeasure before trimming to bind the quilt.

# ADDING THE BORDERS

> ### Tip ✳ *A Slick Trick for Accurate Border Width*
>
> In the next section, you'll learn about border length. But width must be addressed, too. Harriet strongly recommends that each border strip be cut *at least 1″ wider than the desired finished measurement.*
>
> You will find that when you stitch the border onto a pieced quilt top, going over the lumpy seam allowances and not sewing every seam 100% straight will affect the width of the border after it is pressed. If you've added extra width, the border can now be cut perfectly straight using the seam as a baseline.
>
> For example, if the border is designed to finish at 4″, lay the ruler on the seam at the 4¼″ line, and cut along the raw edge of the border. This will give you an exact-width border and a very straight edge to add the next border (if any) onto. Do this for every border you add.
>
> If this is the last border, do not trim it until the quilting is finished. This extra gives you a handle to hold onto when quilting right up to the seamline.

## Measuring for Border Lengths

Measure through the center of your quilt top, end to end, to determine the length of the side borders. If you choose to add the top and bottom borders first, measure through the center from side to side.

> ### Tip ✳ When measuring for borders, do not measure along the actual outside edge, since it's easy to stretch that edge as you measure.

> ### Tip ✳ There are no solid rules about which borders go on first—whether it's sides, then top and bottom, or top and bottom, then sides. It depends on what appeals to you. Look at the illustrations (at right) and notice your first reaction to each. If you feel one is balanced and the other is not, you'll probably prefer to attach your borders in that order, or vice versa. We do recommend, however, that you be consistent when you're adding several plain strip borders to the same quilt.

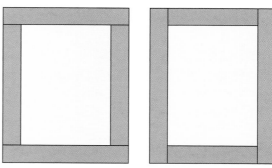

Different effects of border placement

**The side border length** is determined by the measurement through the center of the quilt, from top to bottom.

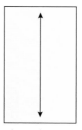

Measure through center of quilt.

The **top and bottom borders** are cut the width of the quilt top through the center, plus the width of the two side borders. Unless there is a strong design reason, it is best to attach the side borders first, and then measure the width from the raw edge of one border through the center to the raw edge of the opposite border.

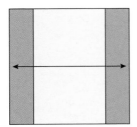

Measure from raw edge to raw edge of borders.

# Cutting Extra-Wide for Accuracy

Many quilters prefer to cut border pieces from the length of the fabric, using a continuous piece for each side. Others cut crosswise strips (selvage to selvage) and piece the strips to get the length needed. (Sometimes your choice is dictated by the design of the fabric; for example, you would usually cut stripes lengthwise.)

If you cut crosswise, you must add together measurements for the top edge, bottom edge, and two sides. You will also need to add four times the width of the border to this total to allow for the extra length added to the top and bottom borders by the width of the side borders. Remember to add ½″ or more to the strip width for trimming, plus ½″ for seam allowances.

Let's walk through this step by step. You are adding a 4″ border to a baby quilt. The quilt top measures 25½″ × 35½″. You need 2 strips the length of the quilt, or 35½″ of border for each side (the ½″ is seam allowance). That equals 71″ of fabric.

The top and bottom borders are sewn on after the side borders, so their length will be 25½″ plus the width of the side borders. If you are adding 4″ borders, that would be an additional 8″ plus a ½″ seam allowance—a total of 33½″. Total inches needed would be 35.5″ + 35.5″ + 33.5″ + 33.5″ = 138″.

*If you are cutting borders from the length of the fabric*, you would need to buy enough to accommodate the longest border (35½″, or 1 yard). If the borders are cut 4½″ wide, you will be using 18″ of the width of the yardage, leaving 1 yard of 24″-wide fabric. This 24″ is now available for strips when making the blocks. When figuring yardage for the blocks, figure 24″ strips instead of 42″, and you will be able to use this excess fabric and know how much more you need to cut as 42″ strips. No leftovers.

*If you are cutting the borders crosswise* and piecing the strips together, divide the total number of inches you need by the fabric width. So, 138″ ÷ 42″ = 3.29, or 4 strips. Four strips 4½″ wide = 18″ (½ yard) of fabric.

The basic formula for borders with *butted* corners is as follows:

**First border length** = finished border length + 1″. (Remember to add the width of the border × 2 for the top and bottom edges to accommodate the width of the side borders once they are attached.)

If a quilt will have multiple borders, this formula continues. To minimize confusion, draw a diagram and write your numbers on it.

# Piecing the Borders

If the borders will be longer than the available strip length, you'll need to piece them. The angle of the seam is a personal preference, but we feel that a 45° angle is the least noticeable. Again, some fabrics will look best with the seam angled, while some may not show a straight seam at all. This will be for you to decide with each situation and fabric. If the fabric is a busy print, chances are the seams will never show either way. However, if it's a solid fabric, the seam can be obvious. Study the illustration (below) to get a feel for what your eye prefers.

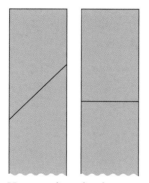

How to splice a border seam

For a diagonal border seam, lay the strips on top of one another, all facing right side up. Using the 45° angle on your long ruler, cut through all the layers. That way, when you position 2 strips right sides together, the angle is correct for both ends. Align the edges and make sure that the offset on either end is no more than your seam allowance width.

When you start to stitch, the needle should align perfectly with the "crotch" made by the two angles coming together. The edge of the fabric should align exactly with your seam allowance guide. Stitch, and press the seam open. If the border edges are not exactly straight, the seam was not aligned correctly.

Placement of seam for diagonal joining

# Adding Multiple Borders

What if, instead of adding one wide border, you want to add two narrow borders plus a wide one? Using the diagram (at right), let's walk through the measurements.

Your quilt top finished at 25½" × 35½". You want to add two borders 1" wide and finish with a 4" border. How do you know what length border strips to cut? The first side borders will be the length of the quilt top—35½" (seam allowance included). Once they are sewn on, measure from raw edge to raw edge of the borders. With the seam allowance added, that is an additional 2½", plus the 25" of the quilt top (minus the ½" of the top's seam allowance). The first top and bottom borders will be 27½". The new length of the quilt is 35"+ 2½" = 37½" long.

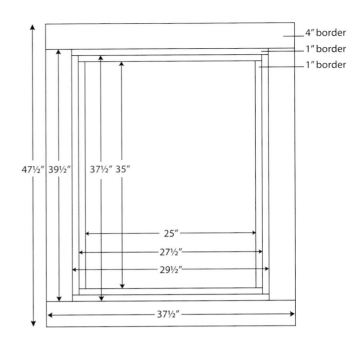

Diagram showing border sizes

You have added the first 1" border to all sides of your quilt top. The quilt is now 27½" × 37½", and you want to add another 1" border to the first 1" border. The side measurement is 37½", so you will need 2 strips 37½" long. The top and bottom borders will need to be 27½" + the 1" width × 2 = 27½" + 2" = 29½".

If the border is cut lengthwise, you will need to buy 1⅛" yard of the second border. If the border is cut crosswise, add the lengths together: 37.5" + 37.5" + 29.5" + 29.5" = 134". Divide the number of inches needed by the fabric width: 134" ÷ 42" = 3.19, or 4 strips. Four strips 1½" wide = 6" (¼ yard).

Keep repeating this process as you work through the wide third border in the diagram. The drawing makes it easy to keep the measurements straight.

**Second border length** = finished border length + (finished border width × 2) + 1".

Continue this process with every border that you want to add.

# Pinning for a Perfect Fit

You've measured your quilt. You've cut and, where necessary, seamed strips together to create the border length needed. Now you're ready to attach those strips to the body of the quilt.

Here is one of our firm rules in quiltmaking: *Always cut borders to size and pin them to the quilt top prior to sewing.*

Never merely take the strips and the quilt top to the sewing machine and start feeding them through the machine. You must always carefully pin the strips to the edges of the quilt top before sewing.

1. Make placement marks on the strips before pinning. Fold each border in half lengthwise to find its center, and mark with a pin. Place a pin at the end edge measurements if you're cutting the border a bit longer than the actual measurement of the quilt top. Find the midway point between the center and end edges, and place a pin at this position on both sides of the center. Repeat this process on the quilt top.

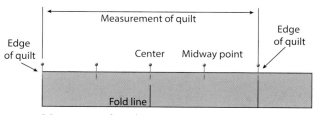

Measuring and marking center points

2. When pinning the borders to the quilt top, we recommend that you work at the ironing board or on a large table. You will be adding 1 border at a time. Lay your quilt top face up. Start at the center. Match the center pin on the border to the center pin on the quilt top. Pin the border in place. Place the heads of the pins alongside the raw edges, making it easier to remove them as you come to them when sewing. Line up the other placement pins on the border with the placement pins of the quilt top.

3. Pin the border securely to the quilt top between these marker pins. Take care to pin the seam allowances down so they can't flip as you stitch the border onto the edge.

4. Take the quilt top to the sewing machine and sew with the border on top, taking out the pins as you go.

> *Tip* ✳ If you find that either the border or the quilt top is slightly longer than the other in the area between the pins, ease the fullness in evenly, and pin carefully. When you sew, place the longer side down. Allow the feed dogs to help ease in the fullness. If the longer piece is on top, you are more likely to get small pleats at the pins.

5. Back at the ironing board, press the seam in the closed position. Fold the border over and glide the iron from the quilt top across the seam allowance, gently pushing the seam allowance toward the border strip. Once the seam is set, apply starch to make sure the border seam is crisp and flat.

6. Repeat Steps 2–5 for the opposite side, and for the top and bottom borders. Once all 4 borders have been attached, pressed, and starched, you are ready to trim and square.

7. If you have cut the borders wider than needed (see Cutting Extra-Wide for Accuracy, page 12), now is the time to trim them to size. Measure each corner with the square ruler again and check for squareness. Make any corrections that are necessary before adding the next round of strips. Keeping the borders flat and accurate is easy if you make them wider and you square and trim each time a round of borders is added.

# Sewing the First Plain Border on Diagonal Set Quilts

*Metro Main Street*

Once the border is cut (including a little extra length to enable accuracy), find the center and mark it; then find the quarter divisions and mark them. Make a mark at the ends at the length needed. The bit you added for squaring is beyond these marks.

After you have prepared the borders, position the raw edge of the border against the outside line that you drew previously in Squaring a Diagonal Set Quilt Top (page 9). Center the border and pin in place. Pin the quarter divisions and the ends in place. You will sew on the border before you trim away the excess fabric of the side-setting triangles. Once you have sewn on two opposite borders, you might want to press the seam toward the border

and remeasure across the quilt top to check that the distances are the same along the length of the borders. If there is any deviation, make the correction now.

Once checked, you can trim off the excess setting triangle fabric ¼" from the seamline. At the ends of these borders, draw a line that extends (on top of the border) the line you drew on the quilt top. Make sure that the corner is square with both the border seam and the drawn line. This line will be the placement line for the next border at the corner. Repeat the process for the top and bottom borders.

*Tip* ✱ Remember to cut each border at least ¼" wider than the correct measurement to allow for trimming once the border is sewn on. You want the border to be exactly the width desired. You also want it to be a straight edge that you can work with when adding the next border. Do not trim if there are no more borders to be added. Once the quilting is finished, you can trim and clean up the edge before binding.

# Making Mitered Corners

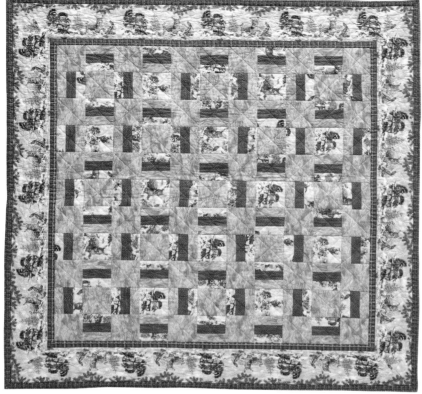

*Woodland Winter*

It is truly a personal choice as to whether mitered or butted corners are best on a quilt, unless you're using a stripe or other directional print. Stripes really frame the quilt nicely when mitered. Mitered corners do take more fabric and more time, but the results can be well worth the effort.

**1.** The first step in mitering is to measure the length of the quilt top. To that measurement, add 2 times the width of the border, plus 5″. This is the length you need to cut or piece the side border.

For example, if the quilt top is 60″ square and the borders are 6″ wide, you'll need border strips that are 77″ long (60″ + 12″ + 5″ = 77″). Cut or piece 2 border strips this length.

**2.** Pin securely, and stitch the strips to the sides of the quilt top. Do not stitch off the edge of the quilt top. Stop and backstitch at the seam allowance line, ¼″ in from the raw edge. The excess length will extend beyond each edge. Press the seams toward the border.

Stop stitching ¼″ from quilt edge.

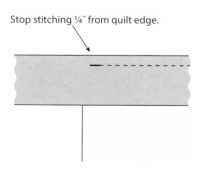

**3.** Determine the length needed for the top and bottom border in the same way, measuring through the center of the quilt to the raw edges of each border. Add 5″ to this measurement. Cut or piece these border strips.

**4.** Again, pin and stitch up to the seamline, and backstitch. Each side of each corner is stitched just up to the seamline and not beyond. The border strips extend beyond each end. Once the borders are on, press the seams toward the borders.

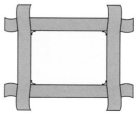

Excess border length extends beyond each end.

**5.** To create the miter, position a corner on the ironing board, supporting the quilt top so that it doesn't drag and distort the corner. Working with the quilt right side up, lay the unstitched end of one border out straight and flat, and then lay the other border out, crossing the first border.

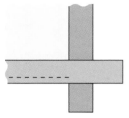

Position border strips for mitering.

**6.** Fold the top border strip under so that it meets the edge of the bottom border and forms a 45° angle. If the border is a plaid or stripe, make sure that the patterns match along the folded edge. Press the fold in place.

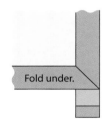

Fold under top border strip 45°.

**7.** Pin the fold in place. Position a 90°-angle ruler over the corner to check that the corner is flat and square. When everything is in place, remove the pins, and press the fold firmly.

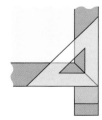

Checking for square corner

**8.** Using a water-soluble glue stick or even Elmer's Washable School Glue (make sure it is the totally water-soluble variety), draw a fine line of glue just under the fold of the miter. Press to set the glue. Now you can fold the quilt top so that the right sides are together. The glue will hold the fold in place perfectly while you sew.

Gluing corner in place

**9.** Beginning at the inside corner, backstitch, and stitch on the fold toward the outside point, being careful not to allow any stretching to occur.

Stitching on fold line—wrong side of quilt

**10.** Once the seam has been stitched, open to the right side and check that everything is aligned properly. If it is, gently tug on the glued area; it will release easily. Trim the excess border fabric to a ¼″ seam allowance. Press the seam open. Repeat for the other 3 corners.

*Note* As discussed earlier, Harriet suggests that the final border be cut wider than the desired finished width so that there is a margin for control while quilting, as well as the ability to cut a perfectly straight and even final border after quilting. When figuring yardage for the borders, don't forget to add 1″ to 2″ to the width of the final border to accommodate this situation.

# Making Borders with a Pieced Design

Pieced borders can add a lot of interest to the edges of your quilt tops. The potential for pieced border patterns seems endless. Any pieced block that you design or choose for your quilt contains elements that can be used for a pieced border. These borders can be as simple as squares sewn side by side or can be extremely complex.

When choosing borders, we personally prefer to work everything out on graph paper. There are several ways to approach this to keep it as simple as possible.

You can start by designing the border at the same time you plan the quilt top. If you work out the complete top on graph paper, a lot of the guesswork is taken out of your quiltmaking. Problem areas and filling spaces can be worked out and solved before you cut and piece anything. We can't stress enough how important precise piecing is to the planning and executing of pieced borders. You can imagine how difficult it would be to plan a quilt border to scale and then find that the blocks that determined that scale are not accurate. You would have a very hard time making it all fit.

You might want to design the border first, work out the corners, and then fill in the interior of the space with the quilt top design. This is also done on graph paper. However, you might find that you don't know what will look best on the border until the quilt top is finished. It will still be easiest if you have planned the sizes of each unit and the layout on graph paper before you start.

Some quilters like to get the quilt top done, then measure the edges, and start the process from there. If this is how you plan to approach the process, be sure that the quilt top is very well pressed and starched so that the edges are flat and even, both sides are exactly the same length, and the top and bottom are the same width. You will need to do this whether you are working with graph paper or not.

Measure the length of the sides of the quilt top. Next, determine the size of each unit in the border—the repeat length. This is generally relative to the grid size used within the quilt top for the blocks. Divide the unit length into the border length needed. You are hoping that the unit divides evenly. The tricky part is to get both the top and bottom borders, as well as the side borders, to fit evenly. This is where working it out on graph paper can help you determine if you need a small strip border to work as a spacer to get the numbers to work happily for you. Don't worry about the corners at this point. They will be the size determined by the width of the border pieces.

If you cannot divide the number evenly, an easy way to handle the situation is to use a spacer (a different design unit) in the center of each of the sides. This will allow you to keep the original unit to size and fill in the gap with something else. Square-in-a-square blocks work really well for this. They don't have to be square but can take on the shape of diamonds of any angle to fill the space.

You will find that the spacing will not always come out exact, but there might be only 1⁄16″ or 1⁄8″ left over. This tiny amount can be eased in as you sew the borders onto the quilt top. Anything up to 1⁄4″ can be done this way; anything larger will need to be drafted to add a spacer or change the size of the unit. Easing in too much will cause the outside edge of the border to have a wave that will always be a problem.

# Tips for Planning Pieced Borders

Here is a list of possible cures to compensate for differences between the size of the quilt top and the length of the desired border.

• When planning a pieced border, the easiest way to begin is to repeat units that are the same size as the quilt block or the individual units within the block.

Repeated elements from within quilt top

• Another approach is to add a small strip border to the edges of the quilt top before you add the pieced border. If the edges of the quilt top do not divide out evenly for the size of the units in the pieced border, this strip can add the additional length and width to accommodate the size of the pieced border. This is easier than trying to change the size of the pieced units.

• If you are using blocks that have pieces that interact and create new shapes when they are joined together, you can draw off these newly formed shapes. Draw 4 repeated blocks that represent the corner of the quilt. Draw units in the border area that complete the shapes on the outer edge of the blocks. The remaining space in the border can be left plain, or you can add more shapes as you like.

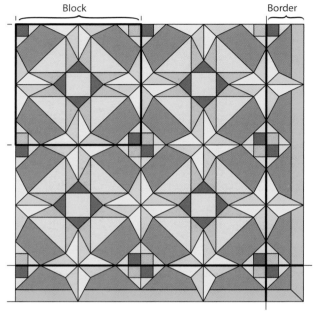

Block elements used to fill in spaces

• When the quilt top is not a square, there may not be a number that works equally for both the side measurement and the top and bottom measurement. A solution may be to add different-sized strips to the sides and the top and bottom of the quilt top.

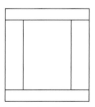

Different-sized strips for top and bottom

• Adding a design element that relates to the pieces in the border but is a size that takes up the different space repeat, is one of the easiest methods for making borders fit.

Adding different element for spacer

- Spacers of background fabric added equally to either end of a pieced border are commonly seen on antique quilts. This is an easy way to add length to a short border.

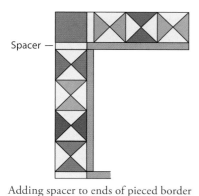

Spacer —

Adding spacer to ends of pieced border

- Corners can be troublesome. Not all designs turn corners easily. One solution is to add a pieced block that is separate from the border design.

It can be related by using the same shapes in the border but in a different configuration.

Changing corner to pieced block

- Work on graph paper to plan border combinations that work within the scale of your quilt design. Work with different numbers of borders, adding a narrow strip border between different borders or changing the size of the grid or the number of repeats.

2″
4″
2″

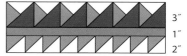

3″
1″
2″

Changing grid sizes and/or adding strips

## Tips for Sewing Pieced Borders

- Accurate cutting, precise sewing, and well-honed ironing skills are needed to make great pieced borders. Handle the pieces carefully to avoid stretching edges that might not be on the straight grain.

- Measure and remeasure as you proceed with the border. Tiny adjustments can be made without showing if they are made equally as you go.

- If you wait until the entire border is pieced, it is usually obvious where the corrections have been made. A tiny bit larger or smaller seam taken every once in a while is hardly noticeable, if at all.

- Even though we really push starch throughout all the projects, take it easy when pressing borders. If the seams and fabric are set with starch, it can be hard to ease the border onto the quilt top if needed.

- Pins are critical to placing the border on the edge equally. Distribute any fullness equally along the entire edge.

- Pieced borders that are on the far outside edge of the quilt can be very difficult to keep straight. If your design allows, add a straight strip border on the outermost edge or, at the very least, keep the straight grain on the outside edge of each pieced unit.

## Pieced Side and Corner Triangles

*Card Trick*

If you find that your quilt lacks pizzazz and the edges just seem to sit there, you might want to consider using pieced side and corner triangles.

When designing the triangles, you can use either two or three fabrics. The same fabric can be repeated on both sides of an inset strip, or a different fabric can be used on either side of the inset strip. At this point, auditioning on the design wall really helps.

Fabric options for triangles

This is also a wonderful place to position small stripes. There is so much interest in many of the stripes available, but quilters tend to have trouble knowing where to use them. Windowpaning, small borders, and sashing are great places to let stripes shine.

## Side-Setting Triangles

Measuring for the side triangles makes great use of the Creative Grids Side Set Triangle Ruler. You can use this see-through ruler to figure how large to make the triangles, as well as where to place the inset strip, at the design wall. You will want to do this before you sew the rows together, as these triangles are added as you make the rows.

The ¼″ seam allowance is also marked on the ruler. You might need to make a light mark on one of the blocks at the end of the row to mark the seam allowance. Place the ¼″ ruler line on top of the block's seamline. Use the cross lines of the ruler to determine where you want the strip to be in relation to the corner of the pieced blocks.

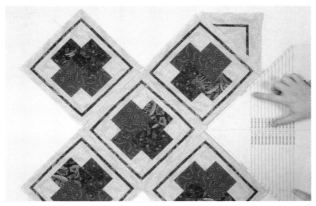

Position ruler on design wall.

The width of the strip you need for the point of the triangle is the measurement from the ¼″ mark at the point of the ruler to the line where you chose to place the accent strip. Be sure to add ¼″ for a seam allowance allotment to both sides of this strip.

Cut the accent strip to the width that you have decided looks best for your project and color choices.

The outside strip is also measured from the Side Set Triangle Ruler. Position the ruler on the design wall and measure out from the accent strip line to however far you want the triangles to extend and float. Add a ½″ seam allowance to this measurement. Now you know what size triangle is needed to fill the position and extend out from the corner of the blocks.

You can also do the planning on graph paper to double-check your measurements. We used eight-to-the-inch graph paper. The strip is 42 squares long, and each square equals 1″. With the graph paper, you can draw in any size triangle and see how many you can get from one strip. You can also see how wide you need the strips to be on either side of the accent strip.

To determine the number of strips it will take to accommodate these triangles, you need to either waste every other triangle from each sized-to-fit strip or make extra-wide strips that will accommodate cutting from both sides. If you cut only from one side, you will need to measure the outside length of the triangle and multiply it by the number of triangles you need. For example, let's say you need a cut triangle that has a long side measurement of 14″. You will be cutting strips from 42″ fabric, from which you can get 3 triangles: 42″ ÷ 14″ = 3. You need 10 side-setting triangles. Because 10 ÷ 3 = 3.33, you will need 4 strips to get the total number of triangles. This method leaves quite a bit of waste, but it is easier to figure out the sizes of strips to sew together.

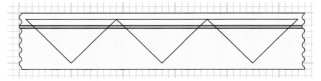

Cutting from one side of strip

If you decide to make a wider strip so you can cut from both sides, it isn't difficult to do, especially when using graph paper. The diagram here shows that you can get 5 triangle units from 1 strip by making it wider.

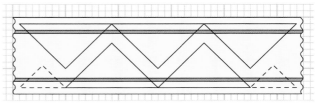

Cutting from both sides of strip

Because each square on the graph paper equals 1″, you just need to count the squares to know the size of each strip. Draw in the triangles and then count the squares. In the first example, the strips are 2 squares (one extra for the margin at the edge), ½ square, and 6½ squares (one extra for the margin at the edge). We added in the seam allowances, so that makes the cut strips 2½″, 1″, and 7″. Don't forget to add seam allowances (½″) to each side of each strip and to the long edge of the triangle.

The second example works the same way. We diagrammed the strip set and drew in the triangles, so we know we have plenty of height to get opposing triangles in the center. The strips count out to be 2 squares, ½ square, 7 squares, ½ square, and 2 squares. The extra square on each outside edge has already been added, so adding the seam allowances would make the strips 2½″, 1″, 7½″, 1″, and 2½″.

Sometimes when using sashing, the corner block is not actually square; it is wider than it is tall. This affects the size of the side and corner triangles. You might find that the accent strip looks best when it is centered exactly in the center of the side triangle. If that is the case, it is very easy to prepare the strips for cutting: You only need three strips, and they are the same width on both sides of the accent strip. As an example, let's go back to the size triangle used above. The long side is 14″, which means the height of the triangle is 7″. If you place the accent strip right in the center, it is 3″ from each side. Now the triangles can be cut side by side without an offset. Add a bit extra beyond the cut edges of the triangle on the width of the fabric strips.

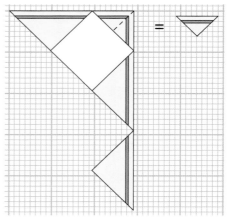

Graph paper drawing of setting triangles and corner

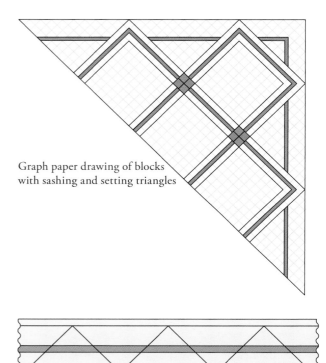

Graph paper drawing of blocks with sashing and setting triangles

Cutting side by side

## Corner Triangles

Drafting the corner on graph paper really helps you determine the strip width needed and the position of the accent stripe. The corner triangles are much smaller than the side triangles, and the stripe is closer to the inside corner.

Diagram of corner

Determine the sizes of strips you need to cut to get these triangles.

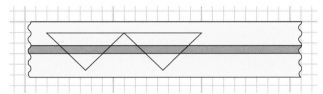

Strips for corner triangles

Counting the grids, you find that the long side of the triangle is 7″. If you are careful when placing the large triangles on the strips you made for them, you can likely get 2 corner triangles out of the waste at the end of the strips. You need 2 triangles for each corner. If you need to make a separate strip, count out the squares again: 2 squares, ½ square, and 2½ squares would result in strips 2½″, 1″, and 3″.

Piece two of these triangles together to create the turned corner. Repeat three times to yield 4 corners. Carefully match the intersections so that the narrow stripe turns the corner accurately. Press the seam open.

> *Tip* ✱ You might find it more exact and easier to make a template the size you need your triangle to be, with the accent stripe drawn on it for placement. A template allows you to double-check the size and position at the design wall before constructing the strip sets.

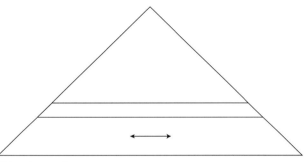

Triangle template

This was a bit of work, but well worth it for what these triangles add to the edge of the border. Congratulations for trying!

Here we have attempted to create an invaluable reference work for the many borders that are used in traditional quilts, as well as different techniques for creating them. We chose to do this so that the borders would be more adaptable to your designing process. When strip piecing and rotary cutting are the only options, several borders would have to be eliminated because of the math and measurement problems the various sizes of borders require. When templates are an option, any size can be made with a bit of drafting, a good drafting ruler, and a calculator.

You will also find that many of the borders are wonderful when the same fabrics are repeated over and over, but the same design adds a lot to the quilt if the pieces are scrappy. Strip techniques limit the scrappy look, but template cutting opens endless possibilities. Keep an open mind and don't look at the clock. It is all about the finished product, but in order to enjoy the work to be done, you need to enjoy the process and appreciate the progress, instead of racing to the end and not enjoying the journey.

The borders are grouped by type: squares, rectangles, triangles, zigzags, and so on. The illustrations will show the process of making the borders, but individual techniques for making the necessary units will not be included. As we always preach, precision and attention to detail can't be stressed here enough. Borders need to fit correctly in length and stay accurate in width throughout their entire length. We will also give you any math formulas you might need for resizing borders. Proportions are important, and often a spacer needs to be inserted to keep the sizing and fit correct.

Because we are working in decimal point measurements and you will need to be rounding up and down, keep this chart handy for assistance in finding the next best number to work with.

## DECIMALS TO INCHES

Once you have calculated the size of your borders, use this chart to determine if you need to enlarge your quilt top by the addition of small strip borders. Whether you round up or down is up to you.

If the answers are minute, you will most likely be able to ease in the tiny bit of extra or gently stretch a tiny amount in to fit. If either of these solutions would cause distortion, you will need to go back and rethink adding that extra strip. The longer the distance to fit, the more likely you would be to round up. The smaller the edge to fit, the more likely you would round down.

| Decimal to fraction | Rounded to nearest ¼" |
|---|---|
| 0 to 0.12" | 0 |
| 0.13" to 0.37" | ¼" (0.25") |
| 0.38" to 0.62" | ½" (0.5") |
| 0.63" to 0.87" | ¾" (0.75") |
| 0.88" to 0.99" | 1" |

| Decimal to fraction | Rounded to nearest ⅛" |
|---|---|
| 0 to 0.6" | 0 |
| 0.07" to 0.18" | ⅛" (0.125") |
| 0.19" to 0.31" | ¼" (0.25") |
| 0.32" to 0.43" | ⅜" (0.375") |
| 0.44" to 0.56" | ½" (0.5") |
| 0.57" to 0.68" | ⅝" (0.625") |
| 0.69" to 0.81" | ¾" (0.75") |
| 0.82" to 0.93" | ⅞" (0.875") |
| 0.94" to 0.99" | 1" |

# Borders with Squares and Rectangles

*Carrie's Beachy Snail's Trail*

Photo by C&T Publishing

The simplest borders are made from straight set squares and rectangles. The piecing is straightforward and the math is easy to figure out what size unit is needed to fit the edge of the quilt top. The following pages contain a variety of straight borders for you to consider.

## Piano Keys Border

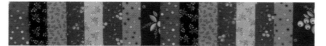

Piano Keys border

Piano Keys is one of the easiest pieced borders to make. It has been used extensively over many years as a way to use up small scraps within a border. Illustrated below is a repeat of six colors. A band of strips is sewn together (see note) then cut into the width you want your border to be, then sewn together end to end, to the length you need.

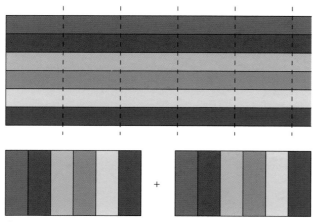

Construction process

> *Note* 🌱 Don't forget all you have learned about accuracy. In order for the borders to fit, each finished unit needs to be the exact measurement. This is achieved by cutting and sewing accurately, but even more important is ironing and starching correctly, trimming each strip as it is added, and measuring the final unit to check for the correct measurement.

You can alternate just two colors for a true piano key look.

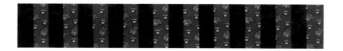

For a contemporary look, try shading the colors from light to dark.

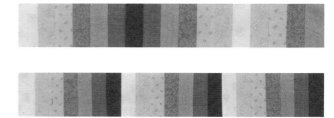

You can mix up the widths of the strips with random measurements.

Even more exciting is creating a scrappy look. Instead of the bands from the same color repeats, use random colors and shorter strips to get the most variety.

This border is very easy to make fit any edge. You can change the width of the strip and the width of the border very easily. Not a lot of math or fitting involved.

As for corner treatment, you can run the strips off the edge (which was very common on antique quilts), use a plain square in the corner, miter the corner, add a fussy-cut fabric motif, or any of myriad ideas. This border is very versatile.

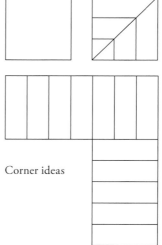

Corner ideas

# Checkerboard (or Four-Patch) Border

Similar to Piano Keys, checkerboards can come in many variations. This is a very graphic border if the fabrics are high in contrast, but can also be very subtle with close-value color choices. These borders are made of alternating squares, generally of just two fabrics. For a scrappy look, use a variety of fabrics.

Checkerboard border

Scrappy checkerboard border

Constructing this border is the same as making four-patches. We suggest that you fan the seams to eliminate bulk and distortion when ironing.

Construction process

The following pages contain a number of different ways to work with squares in borders.

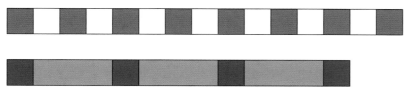

Different spacer sizes

## Rectangles

Following through with the idea of using squares, let's add rectangles into the mix, but still working with the idea of repeats and a checkerboard look.

## Checkerboard Blocks

Incorporating pieced checkerboard blocks into a border is another way to give a lot of graphic impact with simple piecing and math. Below are three ideas to try. These would be most effective in a small grid of 1″ or less.

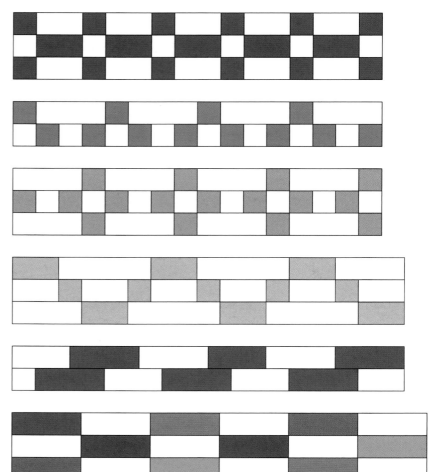

Rectangles mixed in

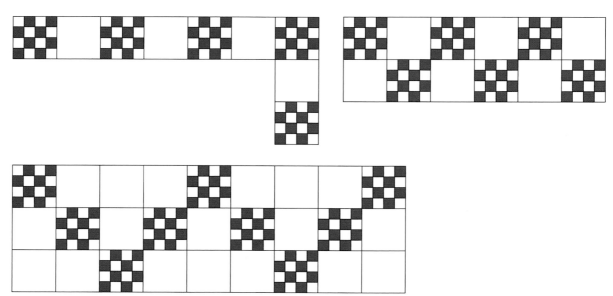

Using checkerboard blocks

# Squares and Rectangles on Point

Two colorways for squares on point

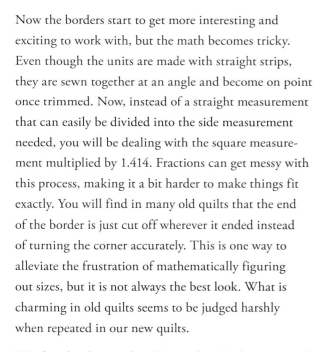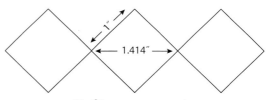

Side border units

Now the borders start to get more interesting and exciting to work with, but the math becomes tricky. Even though the units are made with straight strips, they are sewn together at an angle and become on point once trimmed. Now, instead of a straight measurement that can easily be divided into the side measurement needed, you will be dealing with the square measurement multiplied by 1.414. Fractions can get messy with this process, making it a bit harder to make things fit exactly. You will find in many old quilts that the end of the border is just cut off wherever it ended instead of turning the corner accurately. This is one way to alleviate the frustration of mathematically figuring out sizes, but it is not always the best look. What is charming in old quilts seems to be judged harshly when repeated in our new quilts.

We placed a chart earlier (Decimals to Inches, page 26) that will help you understand the strange decimal numbers you will be getting and allow you to figure out when to round up or down, and how much.

Let's start with simple squares on point. This is a real favorite with most quiltmakers, and we see it in use from the oldest quilts we have (eighteenth century) to today. It is fairly simple to plan and construct, and easy to change the size.

To start with the measuring, remember that the diagonal of a square is the straight side of the square multiplied by 1.414, which equals the measurement from corner to corner diagonally.

Drafting squares on point

1″ = 1.414″ diagonally

1½″ = 2.121″ diagonally

2″ = 2.828″ diagonally

You can see where the math can get a bit messy. When you have a given length that the border needs to be to fit the edge of the quilt top, the sizes generally don't come out as even numbers. There are a couple of different ways to work with this problem.

Start by measuring the width and length of the quilt top across the center, not along the edges. Subtract ½″ from each measurement for seam allowances. This gives you the finished width and length needed.

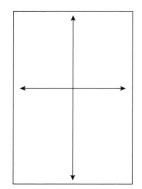

Measuring through center of quilt top

> *Note* ❦ We are assuming here that the corners will be added as an extra block, so we don't have to take into account measuring for the length of the corners added to the top and bottom borders.

If you have an idea of what size grid would look best in this border for your quilt, you can start with that measurement. As an example, say you have a quilt top that now needs 4 borders 36″ long. You think a 1½″ grid will look best for this border.

1.5″ × 1.414 = 2.121″

36″ ÷ 2.121″ = 16.97″

This is a good number, as 0.97 is so close to the next full number that it will be easy to fit 17 squares onto the sides of the quilt accurately. Whenever you can round up or round down just a slight amount, it is doable.

What if your measurements don't turn out so well? Let's work with quilt top measurements of 24″ × 30″.

1.5″ × 1.414 = 2.121″ divided into 24 = 11.31″ repeats—yikes! How do you deal with 0.31″?

1.5″ × 1.414 = 2.121″ divided into 30 = 14.14″ repeats. Better, but not fun.

So, here are your options. Take the time to work with the calculator and see what grid might give you an even number of repeats you can work with, or think about adding a spacer border to change the numbers to ones that will work out evenly.

If you stay with the same numbers, it is known that you need to add a bit to each side to get an even repeat pattern. If you could have 12 repeats and 15 repeats, life would be happier. That means you need to add a spacer border to elongate each side, but how wide should they be?

12 × 2.121″ = 25.45″ or almost 25½″

15 × 2.121″ = 31.81″ or almost 32″

Using this method, you find that a ¾″ strip added to the 24″ sides, and a 1″ strip added to the 30″ sides will give you the measurements you need.

Adding strips to extend measurements

## Chain of Squares on Point

We will start with the strip method, but realize that all the squares and backgrounds will be the same colors. This is not a technique to use if you want a scrappy look.

Once you know what the grid of the square is, use that measurement and add ½″ for the cut width of the strip that creates the squares. Add ¼″–½″ to this measurement for the width to cut the background strips.

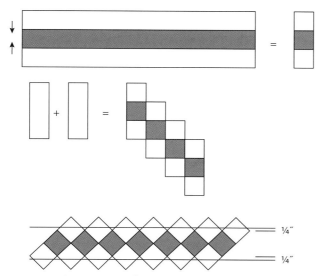

Strip sequence for squares on point border

Sew two strips together, iron toward the color, and starch. Measure the width of each strip and trim if necessary. Add the third strip and repeat the ironing and starching. Measure and trim again.

Cut the strip set into segments. The length is equal to the cut width of the strips. Make sure that you are measuring off the seams, not the outside edges. These cuts *must* be extremely accurate. Join pairs, right sides together, offsetting the segments by 1 square and matching the seams. We would suggest that you fan and iron each pair as you go. Sew the pairs into fours, then fours into eights, and so on, fanning and ironing with each addition. Remember that the edges are bias, so be very gentle with the pieces so the edges don't become stretched or out of square.

Trim the long edges, measuring very carefully off each corner of the squares ¼″ for a seam allowance.

There are two approaches to scrappy squares on point. The math for figuring the sizes needed is the same as above. The traditional method is to attach triangles to opposite sides of the squares, then join the units together. The main drawbacks to this method are working with small triangles and keeping the long side of the triangles true. This edge tends to dip in a bit, not leaving enough width for the seam allowance. We suggest that you cut the triangles a bit too large so they can be trimmed. This method allows you to use a lot of different fabrics for the triangles.

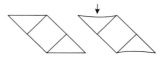

The second method is similar to strip piecing in that you can avoid sewing individual triangles onto the sides of squares, but you will need to sew a strip and then rectangles onto the square instead. There are a couple of extra steps involved, but you avoid having to cut and deal with triangles. With both methods, you have the option of using as many different fabrics as you want.

You will still cut background strips, but instead of sewing three strips together, you will be adding squares to the strip, leaving a small space between squares. Be sure to leave enough room to enable you to square the segments. Cut these units apart and iron toward the square.

Cut the background unit to be exactly as wide as the square.

Next, cut rectangles for the opposite side of the square. They will be as long as the background strip was cut wide, and as wide as the square. Attach these to the opposite side of the square. Iron toward the square.

If you prefer to use a strip, sew the opposite side of the square onto another strip of background fabric, leaving the same small space as before. Cut the units apart and iron toward the square once again. Square up this side as you did the first.

Carefully cut the background even with the square. The unit needs to be straight, square, and exact. Once it is trimmed, offset a unit with the first unit as you did in the strip technique. Match the seams and sew them together. Continue with pairs, then fours, and so on, until the border strip is the correct length. Carefully do the final ironing, and then trim the background away to ¼" from the points of the squares.

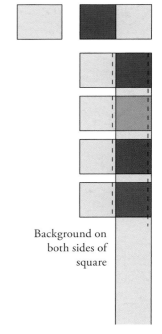

Background on both sides of square

Sewing squares onto a strip of background fabric

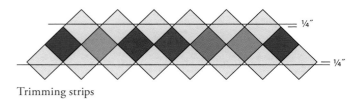

Trimming strips

¼"

¼"

# Mosaic Borders

Mosaic borders are simply more repeats of more rows of squares on point.

The color changes this border lets you do can add a lot of excitement to the design. The following border designs are different because of the number of colors used and their placement. There are several ways to color the mosaic border. The math to figure out grid size is the same as for squares on point, but you just have to measure both directions this time, as the more rows you add, the wider the border gets by the diagonal measurement. The wider the border gets, the smaller the grid needs to be. These borders are wonderful in a 1″ grid. Double and triple are standard, but you can add as many as you need and want. Draw out a line drawing and color in your own colors.

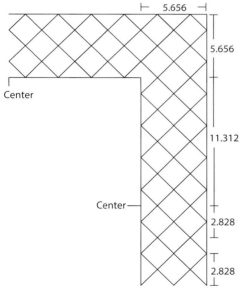

Line drawing of 2″ grid, three-row mosaic border

This illustration shows the corner treatment as well as the diagonal measurements of the pieces along the edge. You can see where the math gives you irregular measurements along the edge. If you add up the totals from the corner to either center mark (this is a square quilt), you will get 16.968, or 17″. If you mistakenly added the grid measurement instead of the diagonal measurement, you would only get 12″.

When attaching the border to the edge of the quilt top, the center of one side triangle would be placed at the center of the length of the edge the border is being added to. This side measurement is 1.414 of the size of the square.

Let's review the math again. First, measure the edge the border will need to fit. Next, determine how large you want the squares to be in the border.

*Example:* You want 1½″ squares within the border. The diagonal measurement of a 1½″ square is 1.5″ × 1.414 = 2.121″.

The quilt top is 45″ square. Divide 45″ by 2.121″ = 21.216. This lets you know that you would need 21 squares on point to fill the space, but you will have 0.216 of a square of extra space. You can probably ease this amount throughout the length of the border, especially since the edges are bias.

Another option is to change the grid size of the square:

1¼″ = 1.25″ × 1.414 = 1.767″

45″ divided by 1.767″ = 25.466—even more to deal with

1¾″ = 1.75″ × 1.414 = 2.474″

45″ divided by 2.474″ = 18.189—a minute amount to deal with

2″ = 2″ × 1.414 = 2.828″

45″ divided by 2.828″ = 15.912

As you look at the possibilities, the 1½″ and the 1¾″ sizes look easiest to work with. Now you will need to make the decision as to which one will look best with your fabric choices and quilt design. As all this comes together, you will need to also consider the width the border is going to be. The larger the squares, the wider the border. If you use a 1½″ grid, the two rows would total 4¼″ wide. The 1¾″ grid finishes to almost 5″. Is this going to be too wide for your design? Sometimes the borders can become overwhelming to the quilt just because of the grid size. How about a 1″ or 1⅛″ grid? Play with your calculator and see if you can start to get a feel for the scale change with each grid size change.

Various color ideas

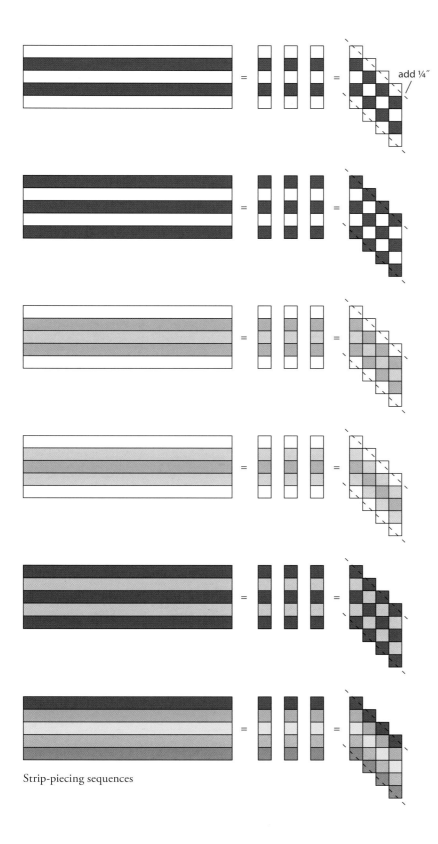

add ¼"

Strip-piecing sequences

**Tip** ✳ When making your strip sets you will need to iron half of the strip sets toward the dark edge and half toward the light edge so that the seam allowances alternate when you sew the segments together.

**Note** ✿ To determine the width of the strips, use the grid measurement plus ½" for seam allowances, not the diagonal measurement. Always add ¼"–½" to the outside (or background) strip for seam allowance. Cut the segments the same width as the strip width for the squares.

## A Few More Ideas

You get to the point where you don't know where to stop when coloring in border ideas. Here are a few more to add to your collection.

Instead of an odd number of units in the border, how about using an even number? Below is an example.

This border is scrappy. It requires using short strip sets and fewer repeats of the same color combinations. It could also have more random color placement, making it even scrappier.

Changing the color of the outside units to blend with the fabrics they are sewn next to can give a floating effect to the row of squares. The color of the outside units can be used to frame or blend, whichever you need it to do in its position in the quilt.

Instead of plain blocks, use Four-Patch blocks in the border.

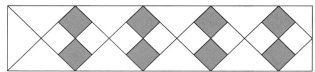

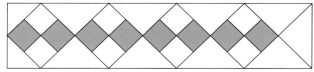

The position of the color can impact the effect of the design.

Once the four-patches are constructed, join them together using spacers. Cut strips of the background fabric the width of the unfinished four-patch units. Cut these strips into segments twice as long as the four-patch units. Sew the four-patches to the ends of the segments. Cut at a 45° angle equidistant between the seamlines. Attach the end piece of the last segment back to the beginning of the strip.

Turn the sections on end and stitch edge to edge, matching seamlines. Square the ends. This is a great way to add variety to the edges of the border. Because it is constructed with segments instead of strips, the segments can be scrappy, giving you a chance to use a large variety of fabrics.

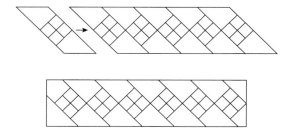

Try using Nine-Patch blocks instead of Four-Patch units.

Any pieced block can be used with this method, which is so much easier than cutting triangles and trying to get them even at the edges.

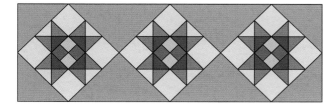

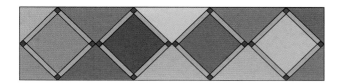

The traditional method for joining these units is to add individual triangles to opposite sides of the blocks, then sew them together. If you choose this method, the measurement for the triangle is the size of the block, unfinished, multiplied by 1.414. That measurement is the size of square needed, cut in half diagonally, for the side triangles. We have found that to cut them larger than needed helps us keep them exactly straight when trimming. When cut to size, there is no fudge room. We also never do this process without using the Perfect Patchwork Corner Trimmer (by Marti Michell). Cutting the special angle at the points makes them always line up correctly.

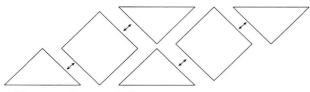

Adding triangles instead of strip sewing

Let's go one step further and piece the triangles to add more interest.

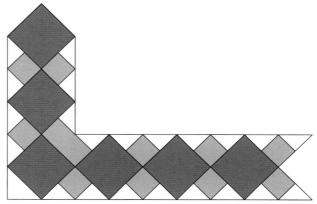

Small and large squares used in border

What if we used Drunkard's Path units in the border? You could really get into some fun color combinations with this idea.

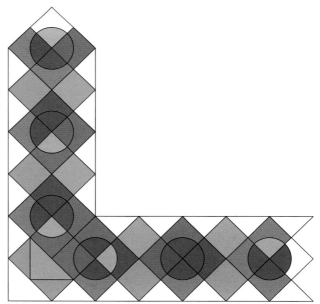

Curves thrown into the mixture

## Diagonal Strips

Diagonal strips can add a lot of interest to a border. This is especially good for using up scrap strips. Below are a few we like.

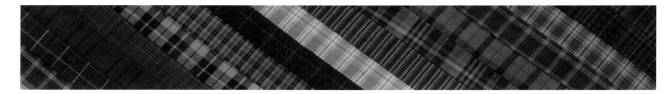

This border is made of strips cut as long as you want your border to be wide with extra added to the cut the width of the strip for offsetting. If your border needs to be 4″ wide, and you want each strip to be 1″ wide, cut the strips 5¼″ long and 1½″ wide. When sewing the strips together, offset the ends by ¾″. Be sure to make a mark at this measurement so that each strip is in the correct position. Once all the strips are joined and ironed, cut the edges from inside point to inside point.

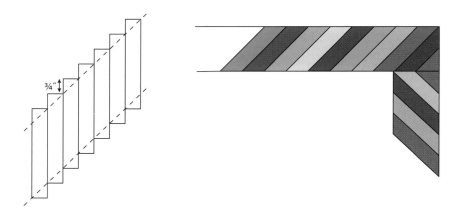

The following borders are striking in quilts. Singles, doubles, offset, and added bands between the piecing all make for a variety of designs to add to your quilt.

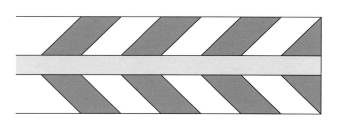

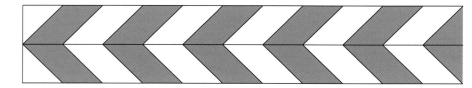

## Strip Sets

The next borders are constructed as strip sets, but with all but the first one, you will need to construct two mirror-image strip units. Changing size for this border is easy, as the finished width of the border is always twice the finished width of the strips. Let's break down the math again.

> *Tip* ✳ This border can also be constructed with half-square triangles. The only problem with half-square triangles is the seam that would then go through the diagonal shape. This would be a design choice as to which technique to use based on the fabric choice and how well it might camouflage the seams.

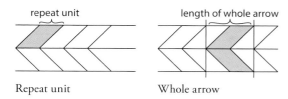

Repeat unit             Whole arrow

The repeat unit along the side of the border is 1.414 times the finished width of the strip. The length of the total arrow is the repeat unit plus the finished width of a strip.

2″ finished border = 1½″ cut width of strip = 1″ finished width of strip × 1.414 = 1.41″ repeat + 1″ (finished strip) = 2.41″ length of complete arrow

3″ finished border = 2″ cut width of strip = 1.5″ finished width of strip × 1.414 = 2.12″ repeat + 1.5″ (finished strip) = 3.62″ length of complete arrow

4″ border width = 2½″ cut width of strip = 2″ finished width of strip × 1.414 = 2.83″ repeat + 2″ (finished strip) = 4.83″ length of complete arrow

When constructing the strip sets, be sure to turn one around and cut from the opposite angle to create a mirror image when the segments are sewn together.

> *Tip* ✳ To save a bit of fabric, stairstep each strip unit. Measure in the distance of the finished width of the strip and start the next strip at this mark. For example, if your strips are cut 2″, step the next strip in 1½″ from the end.

> *Tip* ✳ Iron the seam allowances one direction on one strip set, but the opposite direction on the second strip set that will be cut mirrored to the first.

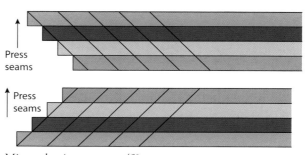

Mirrored strip sets cut at 45°

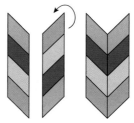

Cut segments turned to create arrows

Once all the segments are cut from the strip sets, sew into pairs and continue until you arrive at the length needed.

Once you determine how wide your border will be and how many arrows are needed for the length, square the end of each long strip by adding background triangles. Cut a square the size of the cut segment, and cut in half diagonally.

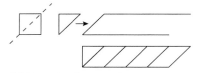

Adding triangles to end

These ends can be used as the center to change direction of the arrows or as a blunt end when a different block is used for the corner squares.

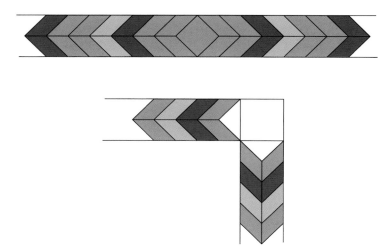

For an unbroken corner, add a corner triangle to a mitered corner of the two borders.

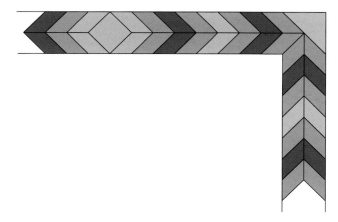

# Stacked Bricks

Another border that is simple shapes cut at an angle is the Stacked Bricks border. This border is another strip border, with the appearance of bricks leaning against one another.

Stacked Bricks

If you want all the bricks to be the same color, strip piecing is the easiest way to go.

Determine what width will look best on your quilt top. The bricks can be rectangles of almost any size you want. Once you determine the finished size of the bricks, add ½″ to the *length* of the brick for a seam allowance. Cut the brick fabric strip this wide (center strip). Add ½″ to the width of the finished rectangle to find the segment cut width. Cut the background strips ½″ wider than the *segment* cut width.

*Example:*

You have decided that small bricks look best for your project—2″ × 4″ finished. Cut the brick strip 4½″ wide and the background strips 3″ wide. The segment cuts would be 2½″ wide.

For smaller bricks—1½″ × 3″—the brick strip would be cut 3½″ wide and the background strips would be cut 2½″ wide. The segments are cut 2″ wide.

If you want a 3″ × 5″ brick border, the brick strip would be 5½″ wide and the background strips 4″ wide. The segment cuts would be 3½″ wide.

With this formula, you can make the bricks any size that you need to fit the edge of your quilt top. On graph paper, try making the bricks narrower than above, but the same length. You will see how the proportions are affected by the measurements. Experiment until you find one that is pleasing on your quilt top.

One thing to consider when choosing your brick size is how wide the border will be with that brick size. Let's go back to 1.414. To get the width measurement, look at the illustrations and you will see that there are 1½ squares making up the width. You will need to take the 1.414 answer and multiply it by 1½ to get the width.

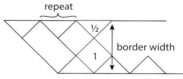

Measuring the width of the border

Below is a list of border widths at different brick sizes:

1½″ bricks = 1.5″ × 1.414 = 2.121″ × 1.5 = 3.181″

2″ bricks = 2″ × 1.414 = 2.828″ × 1.5 = 4.242″

2½″ bricks = 2.5″ × 1.414 = 3.535″ × 1.5 = 5.30″

3″ bricks = 3″ × 1.414 = 4.242″ × 1.5 = 6.363″

The size of the bricks is one part of the equation, but so is the width of the border. Don't forget that the bricks can be made long and skinny instead of in a 1:2 ratio (1½″ × 3″), as we have used in the examples. If you want narrow, skinny bricks, say in a 1:3 ratio (1½″ × 4½″), the border could be wider with narrower-looking bricks. This might appear less bulky for your quilt than wide bricks. Play with different ratios on graph paper and see what pleases your style.

Another consideration as you are deciding on what size to make your bricks is to look at the borders and how the corners are formed when added to the quilt top. The length of the border needed might affect the size of the bricks you decide on.

Each border strip will begin and end with one segment. They are not squared off at the ends as we have been doing on other borders, but instead are either mitered or capped off with more bricks. We will discuss this after the piecing process is covered.

The finished length of each side of the quilt top must be equal to the number of finished segment repeats. Using the size of 1½″ × 3″ bricks, you would start by determining the side measurement of the background triangles. If the segments were cut 2″, the finished measurement would be 1½″. The diagonal of 1½″ (the base of the triangles on the edge) is 1.5″ × 1.414 = 2.121″.

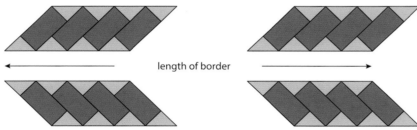

length of border

Measuring for border length

The length of each side of the quilt top must accommodate the number of attached segments in the border. An example would be to have 15 segments sewn together with 1½″ bricks. With the diagonal measurement at 2.121″ and 15 segments, the length of the border would be 31.8″. If you need a border to be 36″ long, adding another 2 segments would fit: 17 × 2.121″ = 36.057″. We like to have the completed border length to within ⅛″ to ¼″ larger or smaller. We know we can work with that to make it fit. By adding the extra 2 segments, we are spot on.

By continually working the numbers, you will be able to get the length border you need, with the size bricks you want, and know how many segments you need to make.

## Construction

To construct the bricks, start by sewing the strips together. Iron the seams toward the center strip. Draw a line on the wrong side of the brick strip down the center. This line will be used for placement of the segments when joining them together.

Sewing strips together

Cut the segments perpendicular to the seams, keeping the ruler aligned with the seams.

Join the segments by placing the top seam of one segment on the centerline of the brick strip of the first segment. This centers the stagger of the bricks. You will need to stagger the sides of the quilt down, and the top and bottom borders up.

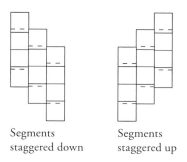

Segments
staggered down

Segments
staggered up

Once the segments are joined, iron the seam allowances in one direction, being very careful not to distort and stretch the edges. Trim the long edges ¼″ from the points of the bricks.

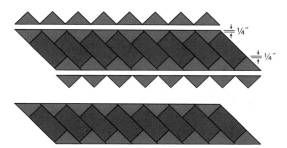

Trimming edges

If you want a scrappy look, use many different fabrics in shorter strip units, then attach them randomly to each other. You can also alternate two colors, or a sequence of colors.

There are two different ways to handle the corners for the Stacked Bricks border. One method will give you two different corners on the quilt. This method keeps all the bricks lying at the same angle on all sides of the quilt top. In this example, the bricks are staggered down in the side borders and up in the top and bottom borders.

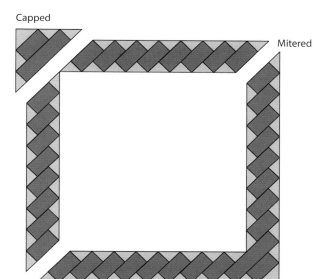

Two different corners

When the borders are attached to the quilt top, the two corners with miters need to have the borders stitched to the ¼″ seamline so that you can create and sew the miter. The opposite corners are capped off with finishing triangle units. To make these units, cut 2 bricks that are twice the length of the bricks in the border and the same width (unfinished) as the border bricks, plus ½″. Cut 2 squares the width of the bricks and attach to the ends of the long bricks. Iron toward the bricks. Make 2 additional brick units the same size as the border bricks. The measurement of the smaller brick plus ½″ is the diagonal measurement of the triangle needed for the corner.

Divide this measurement by 1.414 to find the size square needed. Cut in half diagonally for the corners.

Steps to creating two corners

Be sure to carefully center the smaller brick on the longer brick. Add the corner triangle and trim to ¼″ from the brick points.

The opposite corners are mitered. Carefully align the seams, re-ironing if butting the seams helps you keep them at a true 45° angle.

An optional way to handle the corners is to make them the same, using the capping method above, but reversing the direction of the bricks in the center of each border. This would make each border use half staggered up and half staggered down units.

Cut 4 squares the size of the segment cut. Multiply that measurement by 1.414 to get the size square you need for the background. Cut 4 of these squares. Cut them in half diagonally. Construct the unit in the illustration below.

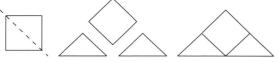

Center unit

Remove one background triangle from one of the border halves as illustrated below. Sew the new unit onto the end of this border half, and then add the other half on the other side of the center unit.

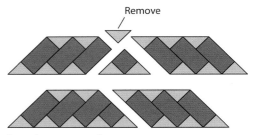

Inserting center unit

Sew the 4 borders onto the edges of the quilt top. Cap each corner with the new units.

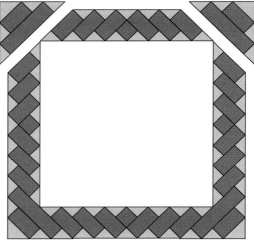

Position of corners

If you want to have fun with a lot of scraps and a totally different look for stacked brinks, consider piecing three-piece triangle units. If you are careful with the color and value placement of the fabrics, you get the appearance of bricks but not the repetitive use of one color. With careful planning of color, this is a striking border.

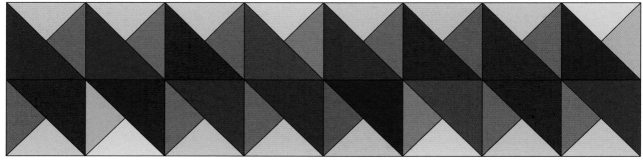

Three-piece triangles used to make Stacked Bricks

# Borders with Triangles

We are introducing simple pieced borders that use half-squares, quarter-squares, three-piece triangle squares, and Flying Geese elements. We hope this whets your appetite for more designs and techniques as you go.

## Sawtooth Borders

This is a favorite border of most quilters and found on endless quilts. It is straightforward and easy to fit onto most dimensions of the quilt top. The repeat is small and there are myriad ways to set the half-square triangles to make many different designs.

The sawtooth consists of half-square triangles lined up on their short sides, alternating light and dark. This border is very adaptable in size, style, and overall design. Following are several ideas for arranging the triangles for this border. Pay close attention to the corner treatment.

### *Single Sawtooth Borders*

The following pages contain a gallery of designs using just half-square triangles. As you are designing your quilt, take into consideration where the seam allowances are, how much they show, and if they will cause confusion with the way you want to quilt the border. When two half-square triangles are placed side by side with the same color touching, the seam breaks the image of a large triangle in this area. If this is a design problem, read on and you will find alternative ways of getting the same shapes with different units.

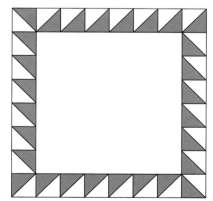

Triangles going clockwise, corners running with direction of triangles

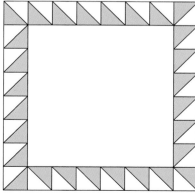

Counterclockwise, corners still running with triangles

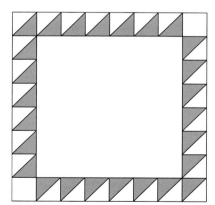

Two different corners with same corners opposite each other

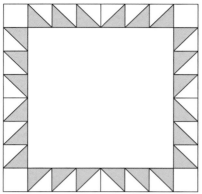

Changing direction in center gives four corners the same.

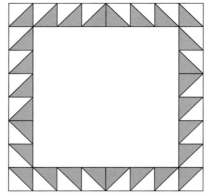

Same idea as on the left: triangles turned the opposite direction

Triangles placed in zigzag formation

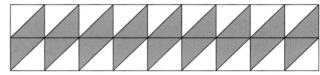

Combining two rows of triangles to get diamonds

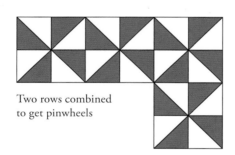

Two rows combined to get pinwheels

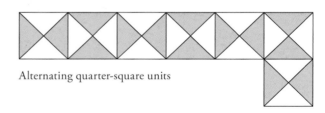

Alternating quarter-square units

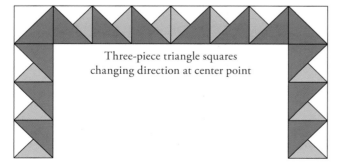

Three-piece triangle squares changing direction at center point

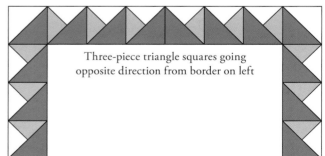

Three-piece triangle squares going opposite direction from border on left

## Double Sawtooth Borders

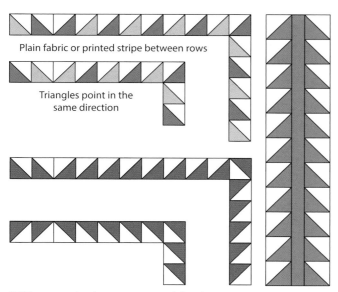

Plain fabric or printed stripe between rows

Triangles point in the
same direction

Different spacing between sawtooth borders

Alternating triangles for a pinwheel effect

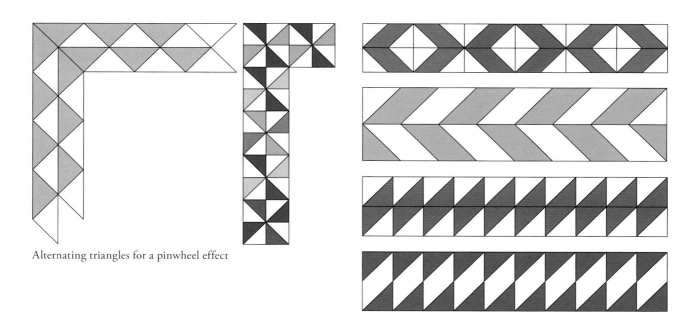

*Note* ❧ Any time two half-square triangle units are placed together to make a parallelogram, the easiest method is to cut a rectangle, and sew and flip squares on the ends to create the angle.

The use of three rows of sawtooth borders around a center can be striking. The size of the triangles can be a factor affecting the success of this border, as too small may appear busy and too large overpowering.

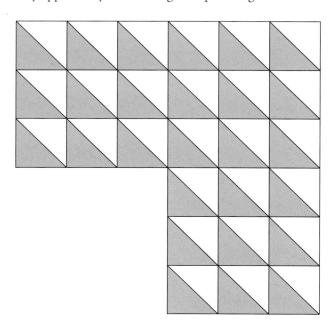

You can mix things up a bit by using a pieced triangle unit joined to a large triangle for a broken sawtooth border.

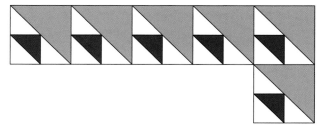

## Dogtooth Borders

The following pages contain a variety of dogtooth borders. These pieces can be combined with half-square triangles and squares in the corners, and can point in different directions.

### Single Dogtooth Borders

Single dogtooth border

Zigzag dogtooth border

## TRIANGLE TEMPLATE METHOD

We prefer this method for borders that are wider than 2″. When larger triangles are rotary or template cut, it is fast and straightforward. The larger triangles fill space quickly. It is also very easy to put together a scrappy-looking border using individual triangles.

This is the most common way to make this border—individual triangles sewn end to end. Without the help of the Perfect Patchwork Corner Trimmer (from Marti Michell), it is very time-consuming and hard to get the outside edges to come out straight and have a ¼″ seam allowance beyond all the points along the edge. We strongly suggest that you take the time to cut the corners with the template to make this border fast and accurate.

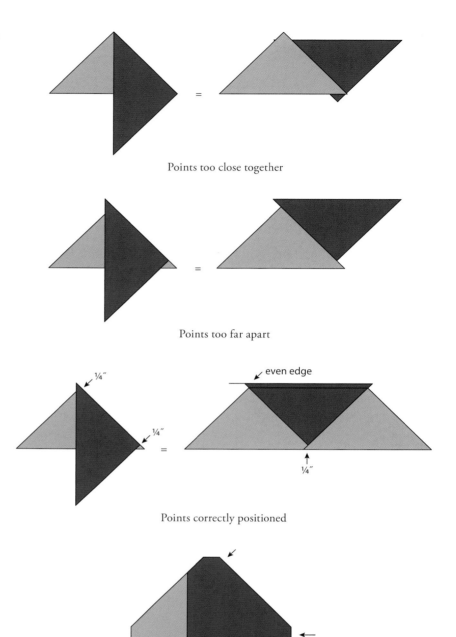

Points too close together

Points too far apart

Points correctly positioned

Template angles that align points and corners for perfect fit

## STRIP-PIECING METHOD

This border can be a very small accent to a wider, stronger statement. We prefer to appliqué the points when they get to 1″ or smaller to eliminate having a seam beyond the points. This will depend on where you place this border. Seminole piecing (a strip-piecing technique) makes creating the more narrow borders easy and efficient. When wider borders are needed, we suggest that you go back to the template method. It is fast and the large triangles fill space quickly.

This is a strip technique. Below is a chart of strip sizes for different widths of borders. If you need exact widths, go back to the triangle template method (previous page). These measurements are odd in order to keep the strip width in easy ruler numbers. To determine the size needed, remember that the long side of the triangle is giving the border its length. After deciding on a corner treatment, measure the quilt top edge and figure how many triangles are needed to fill that measurement.

| Changing Size of Dogtooth Border Using Seminole Technique | | | | |
|---|---|---|---|---|
| Border width | Unit repeat | Dogtooth strip | Background strip | Segment cut width |
| 0.88″ | 1.76″ | 2″ | 2″ | 1¾″ |
| 1.06″ | 2.12″ | 2¼″ | 2¼″ | 2″ |
| 1.24″ | 2.47″ | 2½″ | 2½″ | 2¼″ |
| 1.41″ | 2.83″ | 2¾″ | 2¾″ | 2½″ |
| 1.59″ | 3.18″ | 3″ | 3″ | 2¾″ |
| 1.77″ | 3.54″ | 3¼″ | 3¼″ | 3″ |

Once you choose the size you want to make, cut a strip each from two fabrics the width designated on the chart. We will be working with the 2½″ strip size, giving us a 1¼″-wide border.

Sew the 2 strips together and iron the seam toward the side. On the side you have ironed toward, draw a line ½″ from the top edge of the strip. Cut the strip set into 2¼″ segments.

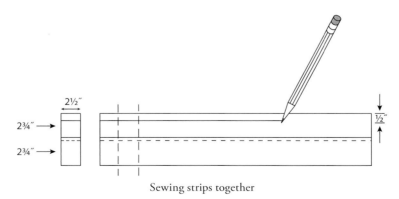

Sewing strips together

Join the segments into pairs, matching the line you drew on one unit to the seam of the next unit.

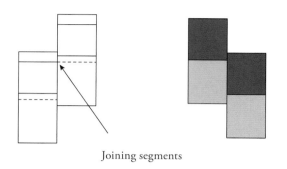

Joining segments

Sew the pairs into fours, and so on, until you have enough for one edge of your quilt top. Iron all seam allowances in the same direction. Trim the edges, leaving a ¼" seam allowance beyond points.

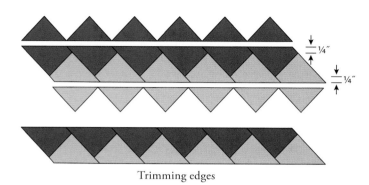

Trimming edges

Dogtooth borders have a ton of design potential, and once you see that they are fairly easy to make, they might become one of your favorite border designs.

When the dogtooth border is made up of two rows, it looks completely different. The first illustration below shows how a zigzag is created when rows are all the same color. This is often called Streak of Lightning.

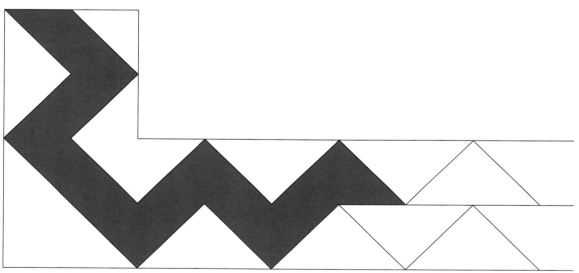

Zigzag border

When two fabrics are used in the same way, a very different look is obtained.

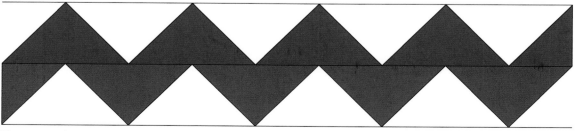

Using two colors

Below are three illustrations of double dogtooth borders with a space between two single dogtooth borders. The distance between the two borders can be any distance you want or need, or a wonderful print or printed strip could be showcased between the two sets of points, especially the two where the points are pointing in or out. Notice the different corner treatments and how they change the impact on the border.

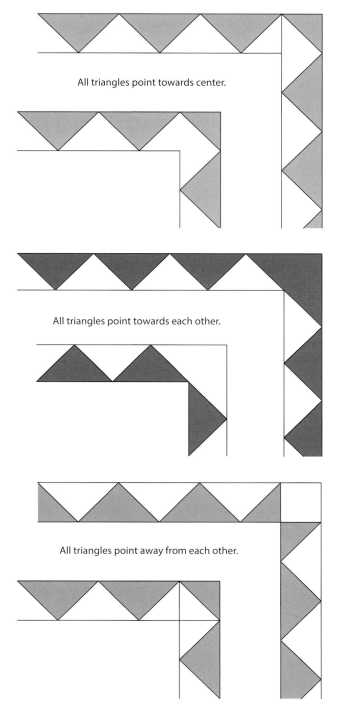

All triangles point towards center.

All triangles point towards each other.

All triangles point away from each other.

The two borders below really add a lot of punch to the dogtooth design. Adding a matching straight border to the inside of the dogtooth border, then appliquéing circles in that space, increases the border interest dramatically.

Color placement and added circles

If one of the dogtooth elements is internally pieced as shown below, you get a totally new idea.

Internal piecing of one triangle unit

# Quarter-Square Triangle Borders

This is a straightforward use of quarter-square units. They can be all the same color or scrappy, and positioned in a straight line or with every other unit turned half a turn. This is an easy border to make in any size from large to small.

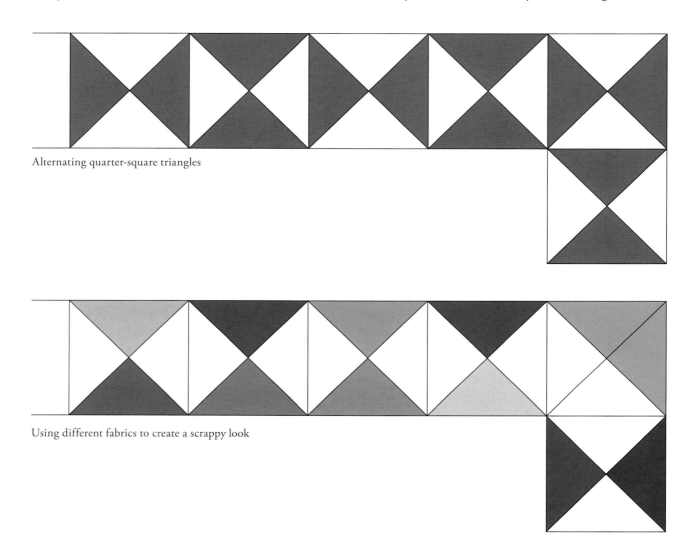

Alternating quarter-square triangles

Using different fabrics to create a scrappy look

# Flying Geese Borders

Flying Geese borders are probably one of the most used and recognized borders in older quilts. These units can be positioned to make myriad different patterns.

# Single Flying Geese Borders

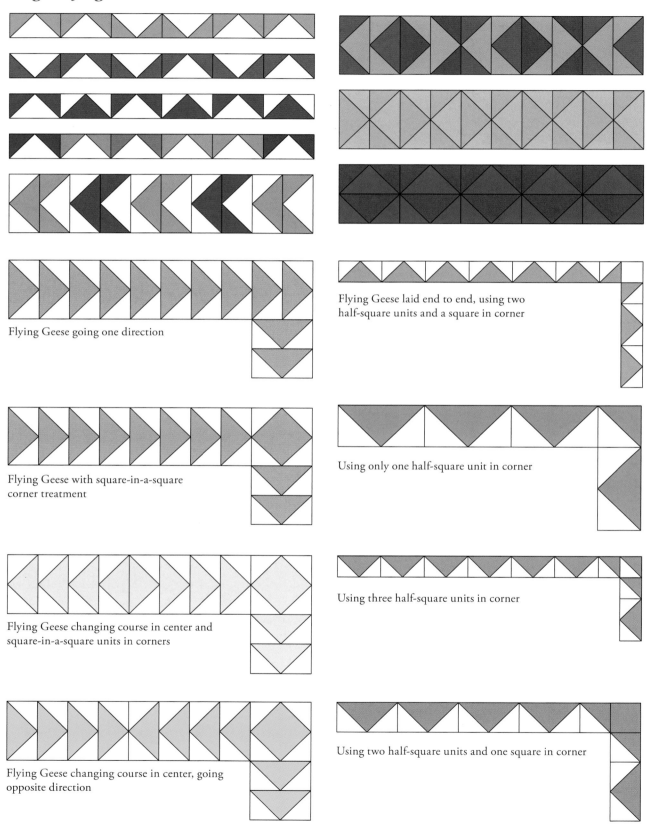

Flying Geese going one direction

Flying Geese laid end to end, using two half-square units and a square in corner

Flying Geese with square-in-a-square corner treatment

Using only one half-square unit in corner

Flying Geese changing course in center and square-in-a-square units in corners

Using three half-square units in corner

Flying Geese changing course in center, going opposite direction

Using two half-square units and one square in corner

## *Ideas for Corner Treatment*

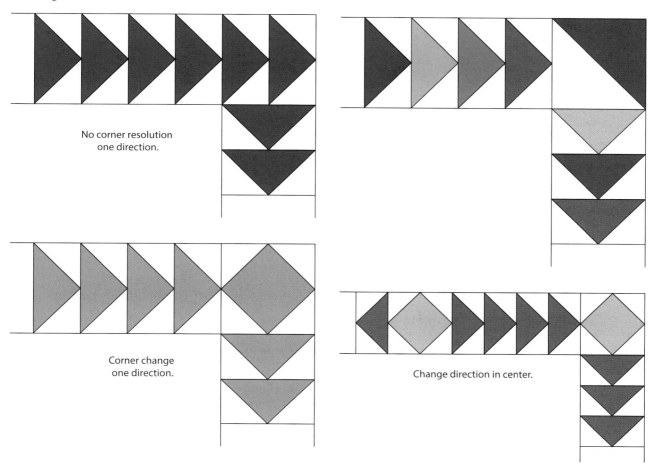

No corner resolution one direction.

Corner change one direction.

Change direction in center.

## Zigzag Borders

Like sawtooth and dogtooth borders, zigzag borders have many variations. We are going to give three different zigzag border techniques: ribbons, peaks, and Streak of Lightning. The strip that makes the center diagonal line is what is referred to as the *ribbon*, the *peak*, or the *streak of lightning*. We are going to refer to this strip as a *ribbon* in the rest of this section to keep it simple. Depending on the width of the border, the size of the ribbon, color changes, and number of ribbons, you can play with this border for a long time and come up with exactly what you need for your quilt.

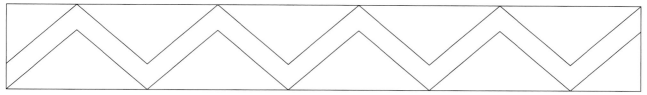

Outline of zigzag shape

Once the angles are established for the zigzag, design elements, colors, and construction techniques can be changed.

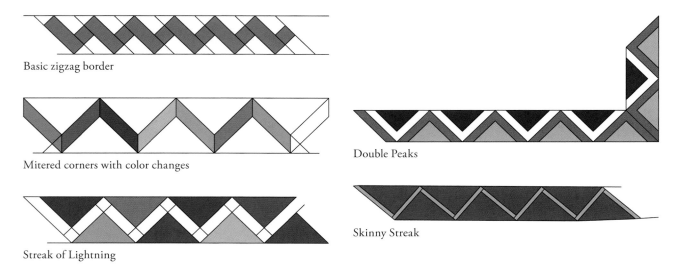

Basic zigzag border

Mitered corners with color changes

Streak of Lightning

Double Peaks

Skinny Streak

There are three different approaches to this border, some using the Seminole piecing idea of using strips and others using strips and triangles. As you look at various elements of the above pieced borders, you can imagine that before machine piecing and all our speed techniques, this border could have been tedious and time-consuming. With strip methods, life is much better.

*Tip* ✳ These borders can be difficult to work out to the right length to enable turning balanced corners. This might be a good time to consider using corner squares as a design element instead of continuous corners.

## Twisted Ribbon Borders

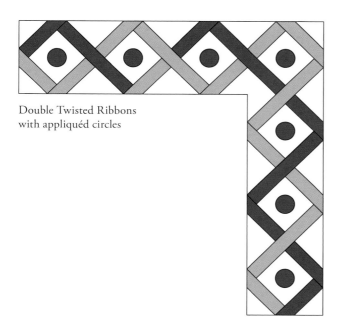

Two-color Twisted Ribbon

Double Twisted Ribbons
with appliquéd circles

This is a quick method when you want a zigzag border, and if you want to give a twisted look to the ribbon by using two different fabrics and the same background. This is a common border seen in contemporary quilts.

This border has to be measured along the side to find the repeat. Because the edge is the diagonal of a triangle, the 1.414 equations are used again. Below is a diagram of where the pattern repeat is.

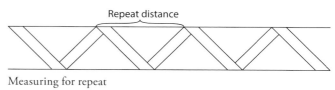

Measuring for repeat

The border *width* is half the size of the repeat. If the repeat is 4¼" long, the border width will be 2⅛" wide. You can see where planning the width of the strips can be confusing with this border because of the addition of the ribbon. We strongly suggest again that you draft out the size you want your border to be and get exact measurements. You can also work it out on graph paper.

Let's try to figure out how to get a 4" border (diagrammed below). We want the ribbon to be 1" wide. Looking at the diagram, we see that along the edge, the ribbon is cut at a 45° angle, so its measurement is 1" × 1.414 = 1.414". We want a 4" border. Since the diagonal measurement is 1.414", half of that would be the height of the small triangle formed where the two ribbons come together, 0.70", or ¾". Subtract ¾" from 4", and we get 3¼". This would be half the length of the diagonal measurement of the triangle between the ribbons. Therefore, if the ribbon is 1.414" and the triangle is 6½", the repeat would be 7.91". If our formula is right—the repeat is twice as long as the width—this would be very close. As you know, we never come up with perfect, even numbers when working with diagonals. This is close enough.

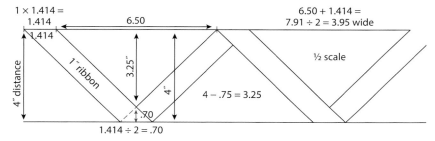

Graph paper showing where measurements are derived

Let's do one more. We want the border to be about 3" wide with a ¾" ribbon.

0.75" × 1.414 = 1.06, or 1"

1" ÷ 2 = 0.5" or ½"

3" − 0.5" = 2.5" or 2½"

2.5" × 2 = 5" (the length of the triangle)

5" + 0.75" = 5.75" ÷ 2 = 2.87", very close to 3"

The repeat measurement would be 8". If you want your ribbon to be 1" wide, subtract 1.414" from 8" = about 6½". That is the long side of the triangle. Half that distance is the height of the triangle—3¼"—plus the 1.414" for the ribbon = 4.66".

Now we need to figure out the measurements to cut the strips of fabric. We know that the ribbon is 1″ wide in our 4″ border, so the ribbon fabric(s) would be cut 1½″ wide. If you look at the drawing below, you will see that you have to extend the triangle units quite a way beyond the edge of the strip to accommodate the angle of the finished edge. We have allowed plenty of extra seam allowance to get a straight cut when trimming. The measurements add up to 5½″-wide strips for the triangle fabric.

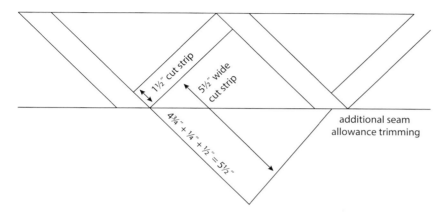

When constructing the strip set, iron seam allowances toward the ribbon. On the wrong side of the fabric, draw a line ½″ above the top seam and ½″ below the bottom seam on the background (triangle) fabric. Cut the segments 5⅛″ wide.

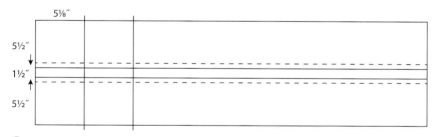

Cut segments.

Cut additional strips of ribbon fabric 1½″ wide, and subcut into 7¾″-long pieces.

Position the top edge of the strip in line with the top drawn line of one segment and attach. Iron toward the strip. Align the bottom edge of the strip with the bottom line on another segment, and attach. Iron toward the strip. If this strip is too short or too long, the stagger will be off, as will be the angle of the ribbons and the shape of the triangle.

> *Tip* ✳ To double-check your math, make a test run and check the position of the ribbon across the segments. The finished width of the segment should be the same as the distance between the segment ribbons when staggered. This area needs to be square in order to create a true triangle when trimmed.

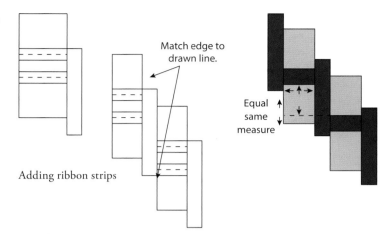

Adding ribbon strips

Match edge to drawn line.

Equal same measure

When joining the segments, stagger the pieces down for two of the borders and up for the other two.

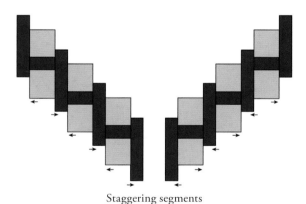

Staggering segments

Trim the long edges, leaving ¼″ seam allowances.

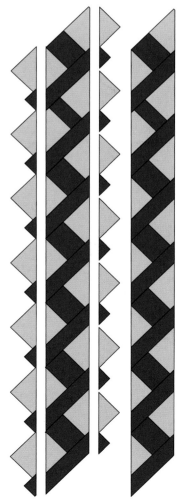

Trimming edges

## Corners for Ribbon Borders

If you thought the math to get the border width has been a bit difficult, you might find that finding the exact length is a bit much. To get the corners of this border to turn perfectly, very careful planning and sizing must be done.

If you look at the illustration below, you will see that each border needs to end with the segment element of the border. When piecing your segments together, start and end with the segment, not the narrow strip.

To check that you have the right size repeat to fit your quilt, divide the length of the quilt top edge by the repeat size of your drafted border. Check to make sure the segment element is at the ends of the measurement. If not, start again and change the width of the ribbon or the width of the border to make the adjustment. Easier yet, consider adding a narrow strip to the quilt top to get that measurement to accommodate the border you want. You can work with up to an ⅛″–¼″ discrepancy.

*Note* 🌿 If you study antique quilts, and especially antique medallions, you will find that as often as not, the borders were not mathematically compatible with the edge they were sewn to. Quilters back then tended to just end the border wherever it needed to stop and cut it off. This can add quite a bit of interest to the quilt, but in today's world, this is not as acceptable as it was once. You do have the option of doing this anytime the math is just too much to bear. You will find that even with the most meticulous planning, things will not fit as exactly in fabric as drawn on graph paper. Just go with it and enjoy the process, and if all else fails, do as our foremothers did and just sew it on and keep going. This is also a good place to use a square corner to end the pattern.

Once you have the borders sized to fit, sew them onto the four sides of the quilt top. Stop sewing ¼″ from the edge of the two corners that will need to be mitered. These corners are simple miters that finish the corner turn.

For the two remaining corners, cut a strip of ribbon fabric the same width as the border. The length can be measured against the quilt top. Add a bit of extra length for squaring the ends. Sew this strip onto the corners. A triangle is added to the corner to square it off. The triangle size is the length of the strip you just added divided by 1.414. This gives you the size square to cut in half diagonally, giving you the triangles. Cut 2 triangles.

Center the triangles onto the corner and attach them to the strip. Trim the strip and triangle to be even with the outer edges of the border.

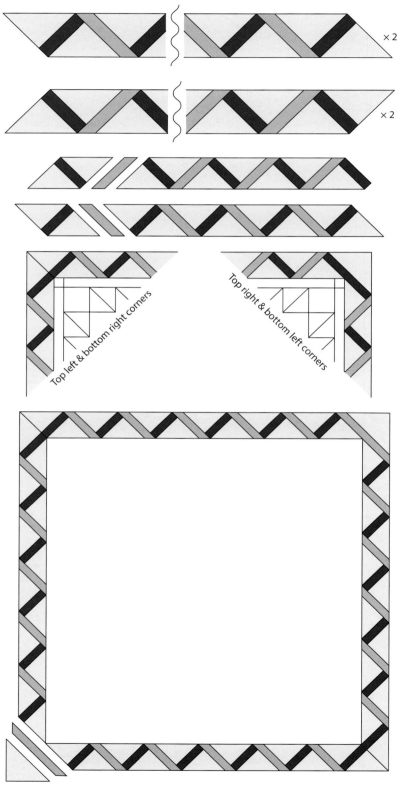

Turned corners

# Basic Zigzag Borders

Strip-pieced zigzag border

This is a bold border based on Seminole piecing techniques. The turns are sharp and close together. The width of the zigzag could be changed to fit your needs with a bit of drafting and measuring. Use the formula in Twisted Ribbon Borders (page 61) to figure out the width and length of this border for your quilt project.

This is an easy and straightforward strip-pieced border. Unlike the Twisted Ribbon, the offset is a given and the stairstep is small. Once you determine the size of border you need, cut the strips to accommodate the background and the zigzag. There are two strip sets needed for this border design. For our example, we are using the dimensions for a 3″ (mathematically 2.82″) border with a 1″ zigzag.

Strip sets for 3″ border

Sew strip sets together, 2 strips at a time, ironing and starching as we always do. Trim each side to be exact and add third strip. Iron the seams of strip set A toward the background and strip set B toward the zigzag fabric.

Cut 1½″ segments from all the strip sets.

Join the segments, alternating one by one, into pairs. Match the bottom seam. Continue sewing the pairs into fours, and so on. When the border is completed, carefully iron the seam allowances all one direction. Be very careful not to stretch the border as you iron, as everything is now bias.

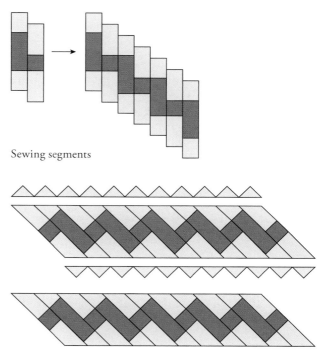

Sewing segments

Trimming edges

If you want to have the corners turn, each border strip must have a segment from strip set A at the left end and from strip set B at the right end. Remember that the repeat needs to be accounted for to make this border fit the corners correctly. Add triangles to the B ends to complete the edge of the border on the outside edge, and trim to a 90° angle. All four corners are mitered.

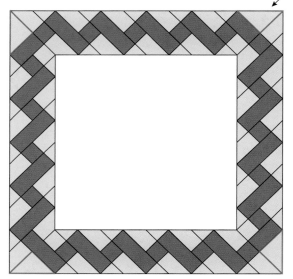

Add triangle

Border layout

## Peaks Borders

*Note* ❦ This is another simpler Seminole technique, but the drawback is the seam through the center of the large "triangle" portion. If you are using a busy print fabric, this will probably not show. However, if a solid is used, the seam might interfere with the overall look of the finished border.

Start by determining how wide you want your border and how wide the ribbon will be, as well as how long you want each peak. This will determine the width of the segment cuts. The length of the peak will determine the width of the background strips. Draft out these sizes on graph paper so that you can determine the pattern repeat. Once you know the repeat measurement for your desired border, you can figure out how many segments are needed to make the border lengths you need. This will then tell you how many strip sets to construct.

Our example has a 1″-wide ribbon and the border is 6″ wide. This method is great when you want to extend the background beyond the ¼″ seam allowance. By making the background strips wider, you can have the edges any width you would like to make them. We cut the sample 3¼″ beyond each peak point on each side to give us a finished border 6″ wide. Cut strips of background fabric 2½″ wide and the ribbon fabric 1½″ wide. Segments are cut 2″ wide.

Sew equal numbers of strips together, stairstepping in both directions (see illustration below).

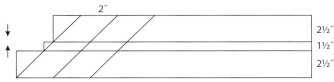

Mirrored staggered strip sets

Iron the seams of each strip set in opposite directions. This enables the seams to alternate when the segments are joined.

Cut the strips into 2″ segments, making sure that the 45° angle is exact with each cut.

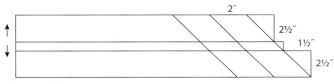

Cutting 45° segments

Stitch pairs of segments edge to edge, matching seamlines.

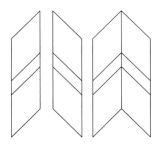

Joining segments

Once all the segments are joined, trim to your desired width from ribbon points, making sure the border remains exactly the same width the entire length of the piece.

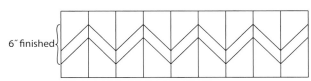

Trimming edges

# Streak of Lightning Borders

This border looks very much like the ribbon borders, but this technique gives you the opportunity to use many different fabrics along the triangle edge, as each triangle can be cut and positioned individually, unlike the strip methods that repeat the same fabric.

Refer back to Twisted Ribbon Borders (page 61) and use the formula to figure out the size of the triangle and the strip that are needed to make your border size of choice. You will only need the first few steps for this technique.

Once you have determined the units' sizes, cut the triangles and the strips from as many different fabrics as you plan to use.

*Note* ✳ The issue of grainline needs to be addressed here. There are two ways of cutting the triangles for this quilt. One is to cut a square in half diagonally, which will result in a long bias edge on the edge of the border. Alternatively, you can cut a larger square into quarters, winding up with all the long triangle sides on the straight grain. Both methods can be defended.

If you need to ease or stretch the border minimally to make everything fit exactly, cutting on the bias would be helpful. As long as you are using starch every step of the way, the bias can be managed without a lot of trouble. Bias is easier to ease and work with when fitting than straight grain.

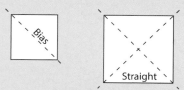

Grainline concerns

On the other hand, if you have trouble with your ironing and tend to stretch borders when working with them, bias would be like a rubber band! Stay with straight grain. This is totally your decision to make.

If you decide to cut straight-grain triangles, use the cut size of the short side of the triangle and multiply by 1.414, and you will have the size square needed for cutting into quarters.

*Example:*

For a 3¾″-wide border, the long side of the triangle is 6″ finished. Add 1¼″ for seam allowances to find the size of the square that is cut into quarters. If you want to find the size square to cut in half, use the 6″ measurement divided by 1.414 (4.24″). That measurement plus a ⅞″ seam allowance (4.24″ + 0.875″) would be a 5⅛″ square, cut in half diagonally.

To construct this border, cut the ribbon strips the length of the short side of your triangle, squaring off the ends. Attach the strips to one short side of the triangles, making half of them the opposite way, mirroring the first half.

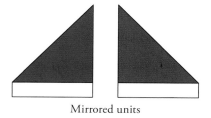

Mirrored units

Alternate the mirrored units and lay out the border. Sew pairs together first. Stitch from the lower edge of the triangle to about three-fourths of the way to the end. Leave this end open for the next step. Iron all seams toward the triangle.

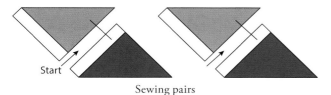

Start

Sewing pairs

*Tip* ✻ We suggest that you trim the long points of the triangles with the Perfect Patchwork Corner Trimmer (by Marti Michell) to get an exact fit when joining these units. There is no fudge room for the ¼″ seam allowance needed along the edge, so very accurate sewing is required.

Align the blunt end of the unit you are adding to the end of the strip on the seam left open. Sew the units together.

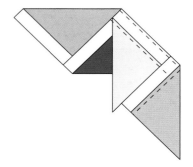

Iron toward the triangle. Complete the unit by closing the seam that was left partially open. Iron.

Close this seam

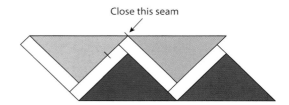

# Borders with Diamonds

## Diamond Borders

There are many variations of diamond borders. Some of the diamonds lie down and some stand up. Some can turn a corner and some can't. We are going to cover four basic diamond borders.

Lazy Diamonds

Diamonds at Attention

Half-Diamonds

Alternating Diamonds

A diamond is half as wide as it is long, so all the angles are 45°. If you were to cut a true diamond, you could fold it in half and it would line up exactly. Don't confuse true diamonds with parallelograms. These "diamonds" don't have equal sides. Two sides are longer than the other two. We are starting with one of the easiest but most stunning of the diamond borders.

*Note* ❧ In today's quilting world, it has become a standard practice to use two half-square triangles sewn together to get "diamonds" for blocks such as LeMoyne Star, Snow Crystals, and Lone Star. The idea is that triangles are easier to make than diamonds. When two half-square triangles are joined, you do not get a true diamond, but a parallelogram. The diagonal seam is 1.414 of the side seams. When this is substituted for diamonds, the pattern of the block is out of proportion. If you have ever looked at one of these quilts and wondered what was just off a bit about it, this is the problem. We will not be taking short cuts but working with real diamonds for these borders.

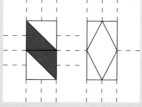

Diamonds versus parallelograms

## Lazy Diamonds

The design repeat for this border is the length of the diamond. Start out with drafting to find the design repeat for the size border you want to create. This border can be any size, but the corners need to be considered when you are doing your planning. The corner treatment will affect the placement of the repeat in the border. Below are five different corner treatments.

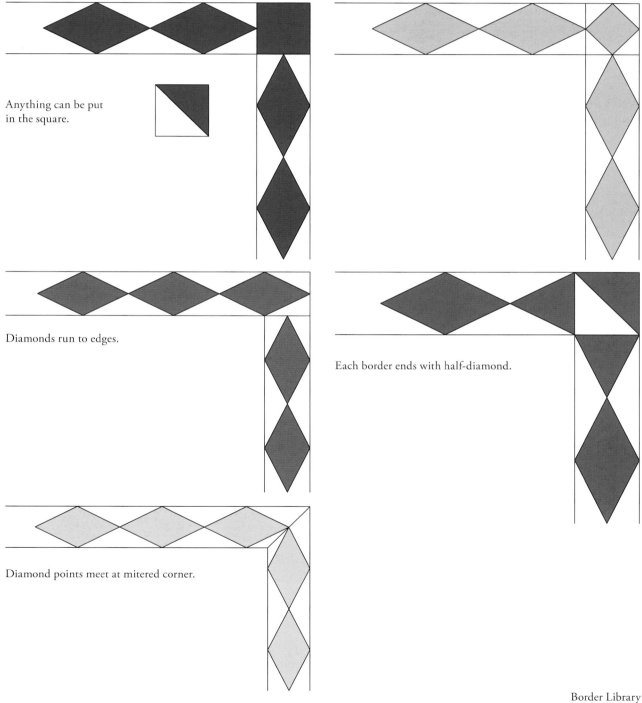

Anything can be put in the square.

Diamonds run to edges.

Diamond points meet at mitered corner.

Each border ends with half-diamond.

The first border example shows the diamond points ending at the edge of the quilt top, so the repeats need to fit into that space, if necessary through adding a small plain border to get the width border you need.

The second border example has the side borders ending with points at the edge of the quilt, but the top and bottom borders going to the outside edge of the side borders. This might be quite a bit harder to make happen, depending on the length of the diamonds.

Border example three ends the diamond repeat with a half-diamond, so the repeat is now the length of the background (also a half-diamond) instead of a full diamond.

Border four goes all the way into the corner, which is mitered.

Drafting these borders onto graph paper to work out the measurements is strongly suggested. Once drafted, you will see what needs to be adjusted or added to make the corners work.

To strip piece this border, figure what size strips you need. The background strip needs to be as wide as the diamond is long plus seam allowances. If we were making a 2″-wide border, the diamond would be 4″ long. If you draw this diamond on graph paper, you find that each side of the diamond measures 2¼″. Add ½″ and you have the width of the background strips, 2¾″ wide. The width of the diamond is 1¾″, needing a strip 2¼″ wide.

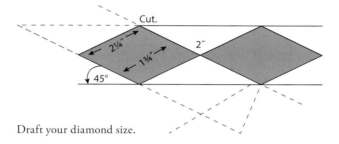

Draft your diamond size.

Sew the strips together. Offset the ends if you choose. Iron the seams toward the diamond fabric.

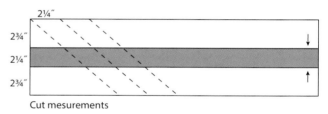

Cut mesurements

Strip set

We recommend that you use a 45° triangle ruler to cut segments. This helps you keep the angle exact by aligning the ruler lines on the two seams with each cut. Straight rulers tilt easily, and if the cuts are not exact, your diamonds won't be either. Carefully cut 2¼″ segments.

Cutting with triangle ruler

Join the segments into pairs, then fours, and so on, matching seams carefully.

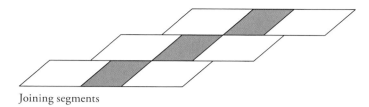

Joining segments

> **Tip** ❊ If you have problems matching these seams because of the 45°, use your Perkins Perfect Piecing Seam Guide to make a small mark on the seam allowance on the wrong side, showing you where you will be stitching from the edge. Use a pin to align both top and bottom units right at the mark. Swing the pin around to take the stitch along one of the ironed seam allowances. This will help hold everything in place correctly. Clover Fine Patchwork Pins can be sewn over, so you don't have to remove them.

Iron all seams in the same direction. This is bias again, so work carefully. Trim the long edges, leaving a ¼″ seam allowance.

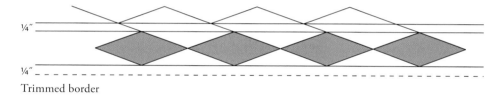

Trimmed border

> **Tip** ❊ For some design fun, try drafting this border as a 60° diamond instead of a 45° diamond.

## Diamonds at Attention

These diamonds are standing at attention on their points. This border can also be strip-pieced. We are working with a 3″ border this time. The drafting below shows where we are getting the sizes for our strips and segments.

Stitch the segments together, matching the bottom seamline in one segment to the top seamline in the next. To square off the ends, add a wide strip of background fabric to both ends and cut square.

Drafting for Diamonds at Attention

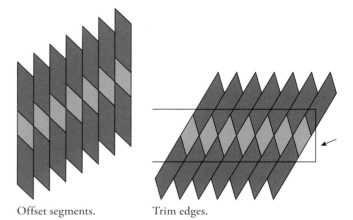

Offset segments.　　　　Trim edges.

Our measurements are 2¼″-wide background strips and 1⅞″-wide diamond strips. You might want to add a bit more to the background width for a little breathing room when trimming. Sew the strips together and iron toward the diamond strip. Check that each strip measures, finished, exactly what it should. Using the 45° ruler again, align it with the seams and cut 1⅞″ segments.

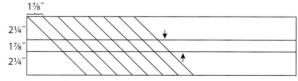

Strip set and segments

## *Half-Diamonds (a.k.a. Dogtooth)*

Another classic pattern is made using half-diamonds.

These diamonds can be drafted in different proportions. As you can see by the illustration below, by changing the ratio, you get short and wide half-diamonds or long and thin diamonds. This could be a real help in fitting a border to a side with odd measurements.

We suggest that you use templates with the points trimmed to fit together the units for this border.

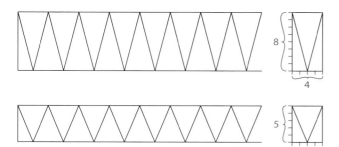

Two different proportions

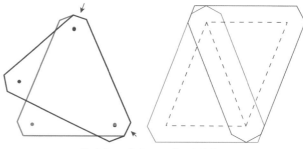

Position of pieces when joining

## Alternating Diamonds

We have dealt with the math in this section with word problems and associations, not algebra. When dealing with diamonds, however, algebra may help you. This border is really based on the eight-pointed star, or LeMoyne Star. You can see where the shape is coming from in this illustration of an eight-pointed star.

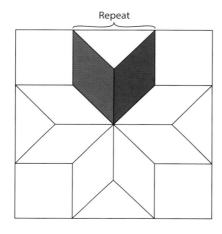

The previous two diamond borders are easier to work with, as the measurements are straightforward. However, when the diamonds are tilted to the side, the drafting is more difficult. Now we need to deal with real math.

Not being good at algebra, I turned to Jinny Beyer's book Medallion Quilts to get a specific answer to drafting and fitting this particular border. If I want the star points in the corners, how do I find out what size to make the diamonds? Her example uses a given size of 42″ × 69″. After dividing several different numbers to find a number of repeats that might work, she found the unit repeat number of 4.245 the best she could do. That would be 9.88 units on the 42″ side and 16.23 units

on the 69″ side. With some fitting and adjusting, that could work. However, how do you draft a diamond the correct size to use in a 4.25″ unit? We can't work with graph paper, as that would give us parallelograms. So she suggests you draft an eight-pointed star into any size square you choose, and then scale it up or down to the size you need. In her example, she drafted an 8½″ square, which gave a distance of 3½″ across the triangle, which is where the measurement for the distance of the repeat unit comes from. Here is the equation to get this answer to accommodate the 4.25″ needed size.

We can now say that 3.5″ is to an 8½″ square as 4.25″ is to $x$″.

$$3.5 \div 8.5 = 4.25 \div x$$

**Work with this equation:**

$$3.5x = 8.5 \times 4.25$$

$$3.5x = 36.125$$

$$x = 36.125 \div 3.5$$

$$x = 10.32$$

Now we know that an eight-pointed star will have to be drafted in a 10.32″ (10⅜″) square in order to get the correct size pattern pieces. You can see that even this is not exact, as rounding up is necessary to work with a ruler.

This same procedure can be used for other eight-pointed star designs, like the diamond border we just covered—Diamonds at Attention. Once you figure out the repeat distance (or the width of each star, in this case 1.5″) you need, fit it into the formula. An 8.5″ star would produce a diamond that is 1⅞″ across its widest point. Therefore, 1⅞″ (1.875) is to an 8.5″ star as 1.5″ is to $x$″.

$$1.875 \div 8.5 = 1.5 \div x$$

$$1.875x = 8.5 \times 1.5$$

$$1.875x = 12.75$$

$$x = 12.75 \div 1.875$$

$$x = 6.8$$

You would need to draft the star in a 6.8″ square in order to get a diamond that was 1.5″ across.

We realize that most of you are blown away by this kind of math, as we often are. We do find, however, that when you sit down in quiet and work the equation repeatedly with different sizes, you start to see the logic in the whole thing. The answers derived from this type of drafting and math often result in needing to use templates if the measurements aren't ruler friendly, eliminating speed strip piecing. If all else fails, the way around this situation is to add small plain borders to grow the quilt top to a size that works with strip-piecing measurements.

When scouring dozens of quilt books to find ways to draft and construct borders, we were surprised that we couldn't find anything but charts of measurements that were in happy sizes, but no instructions as to how to make special sizes for odd measurements. If we wanted to develop a specific width border, or needed a specific repeat to fit the measurements of a given round of borders, it was nowhere to be found. Not being as sharp as we would like to be with math, we set out to actually do the math and see what happens. Here is our journey.

The edge of the quilt top that we want this border on measures 26.25″. After dividing even unit measurements into this number, the only one close was a repeat of 2″, but that only makes the border width come to about 2½″. That is too small for the appearance it would have on the quilt top. If the repeat was 3.25″, eight repeats would fit great, and it is an even number of pairs, so the corners would turn. Now what?

If we use the algebraic equation, we get the following:

$$3.5 \div 8.5 = 3.25 \div x$$

$$3.5x = 8.5 \times 3.25$$

$$3.5x = 27.625$$

$$x = 27.625 \div 3.5$$

$$x = 7.89 \text{ or } 7⅞$$

So next, we need to draft a 7⅞″ eight-pointed star.

We work through all the steps to get the finished star. This should give us the center unit and the diamond size we need for our border, and to our surprise, it was exact once the star was drafted.

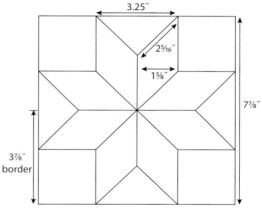

7⅞″ drafted eight-pointed star

Measure the width of the points, the length of one side of a point, and the distance between two points. Here are our answers:

The point is 1⅝″ wide.

The side of the point is 2⁵⁄₁₆″ long.

The distance between two points is 3¼″.

We then copied one of the design elements and drew it on a fresh sheet of graph paper to create the border.

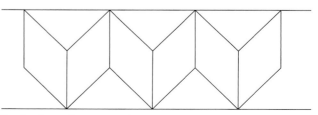

Border drawn from star unit

Now all that is left is to draw in the lines that represent the strips of background and diamond fabric for strip piecing.

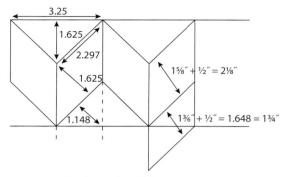

Getting strip width measurements

We now know that the background strips are 1³⁄₁₆″. The way we know this is that the background strip has to accommodate the background triangle. If we know that the distance between the star points is 3¼″, the height of the triangle is 1⅝″. Multiply 1.625″ by 1.414 to get 2.297″ (the distance between the triangle point and the star point). This is also the length of each side of the star. The height of this small triangle is half of 2.297″, or 1.149″, or 1³⁄₁₆″. Add ½″ for seam allowances and you get 1.648″, or close to 1¾″. The diamond strip is 1⅝″, or 2⅛″ cut.

Because the diamonds mirror each other and generally are made of two different colors, you will need two different strip sets. The strip sets will be cut at opposite angles to one another. Iron seam allowances toward the center strip on one set and out toward the background on the second strip set. Remember to trim before adding the third strip.

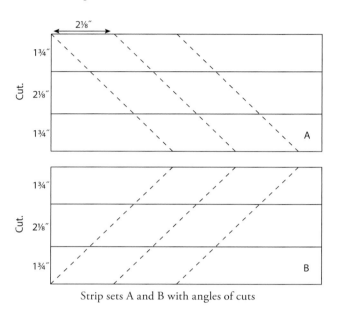

Strip sets A and B with angles of cuts

Once the segments are cut, sew one of each set together to form pairs and continue until your border is the right length. Iron seam allowances carefully to one side or open. Trim long sides, leaving ¼″ for seam allowances.

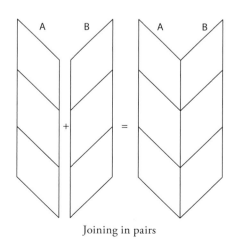

Joining in pairs

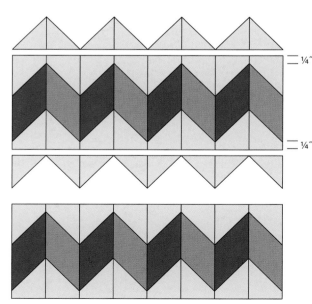

Trimming edges

Looking at the finished product, you see that we once again have the seam down the center of the side triangles because of the strip piecing method. If this is not pleasing to you because of the distraction the line can cause when quilting, or it is not true to the era of the quilt you are making, you can piece these units together using Y-seams as we do for constructing a LeMoyne Star.

Y-seam border

The first step of making a LeMoyne Star is to join two diamonds with a side triangle. These units make the border. These pieces can be cut with rotary measurements or using templates if you had to draft a non-ruler-friendly eight-pointed star for size. Trim the corners with the Corner Trimmer before you start to sew.

You will construct as many Y-units as you need per border, then join them together with triangles. Be sure to sew to the seamline only when you join the Y-units together so the triangle can be set into the point.

Start by laying out the three pieces needed for the units to the right of your machine. Stack as many units on top of one another as you need.

The Y-unit we are making

Pick up the triangle on the top of the pile and place it on the left diamond, right sides together. Align the edges and corners exactly. This is where the Corner Trimmer saves the day. Stitch the two pieces together with the triangle on top. This seam is stitched edge to edge.

Stitch triangle to left diamond.

Do not clip threads or cut units apart. Continue to chainstitch the remaining units in the two piles until they are all joined. Clip the units apart and iron each seam allowance toward the diamond. Return the units to the same position they were in before sewing, where the remaining diamond is.

Pick up one of the units you just completed and place the right diamond on the top of the pile, right sides together with the triangle, again aligning the points of both exactly and making sure the edges are perfectly even.

Adding second diamond

Turn the unit over so that the triangle is on top and you can see the previously sewn seam. Sew from the edge of the triangle to the stitching, and stop. Be careful not to go one stitch beyond the stitching.

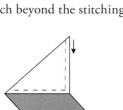

Sewing from triangle side

Continue until all units are joined. Iron seam allowances toward the triangle.

Next, fold one unit in half, right sides together, and align the edges of the diamonds. The triangle will be folded in half. Be sure that the points of the diamonds and the triangles, as well as all the outside edges, are even. Pin in place if you feel the need to hold the layers together tightly.

Folded in half

Pull the seam allowance down and out of the way before sewing. Sew this seam from the outer edge of the diamond point down to the previous stitching. Repeat with all remaining units. Iron seam allowance toward the left diamond (looking at the right side), ironing from the right side of the fabric.

Lay out the units to make the border length and place the remaining triangles. You will continue with the process you just completed, adding in the same manner each triangle that is not in place yet. Position the triangle on top of the left diamond and sew the seam end to end. Iron the seam toward the diamond. Position the triangle onto the next unit. With the triangle on top, stitch to the stitched seam. Iron the seam allowance toward the triangle.

Fold the two units in half and align all the seams. Stitch the diamonds together. Repeat until all the units are joined.

Join two Y-units, sewing from the triangle edge and stopping at the seamline where the two diamonds meet. Iron seam allowance to one side. Position the triangle in the opening and lay it on top of one of the diamonds, right sides together, aligning all the edges and the points exactly. Stitch to the stitching you just completed. Iron, and then flip the unit over and attach the opposite side of the triangle. Iron again. If everything aligned properly, you will have a ¼″ seam allowance beyond all the edge points for your border.

Backside of completed units

This would be a great border if it was scrappy, and this technique would easily accommodate the fabric changes.

## Delectable Mountains

We have added a few illustrations of Delectable Mountains borders. These designs show up in many of the nineteenth-century medallion quilts and are quite striking.

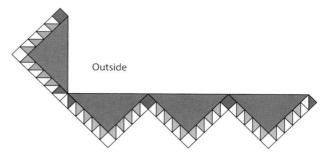

Outside

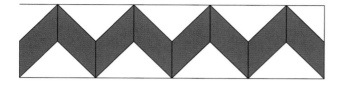

Units positioned end to end

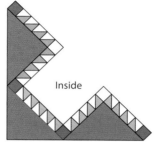

Inside

Inside and outside corner designs

Each mountain ends with separate triangles.

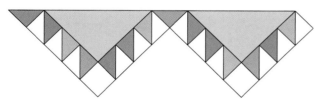

Units are sharing a triangle.

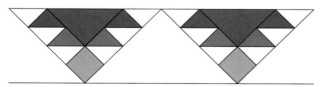

Horizontal-seamed half-square triangle instead of vertical

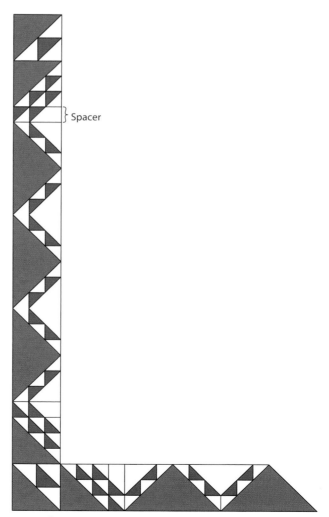

Spacer

Unusual spacing at corners makes nice turn.

# Gallery of Borders with Angles

We have illustrated borders that contain elements of 60° and 45° diamonds, as well as hexagons and triangles. The entire block, or a combination of its parts, is repeated to make the border. Dissecting blocks to get various shapes that correspond with your vision of the quilt is a fun way to design an original border. We suggest that you go on a hunt for unique borders that inspire you by looking through books, magazines, and photos of all types of quilts. Start a file of ideas that will help jump-start a project later.

Following is a gallery of pieced borders using 60° and 45° diamonds, as well as hexagons and triangles. We have included simple to complicated designs. Can you come up with any more? Can you create different corners?

## 60° Angles

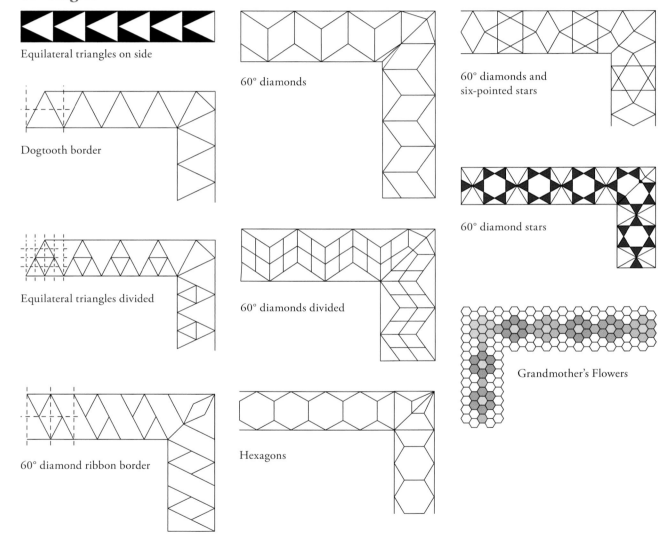

Equilateral triangles on side

Dogtooth border

Equilateral triangles divided

60° diamond ribbon border

60° diamonds

60° diamonds divided

Hexagons

60° diamonds and six-pointed stars

60° diamond stars

Grandmother's Flowers

## 45° Diamonds

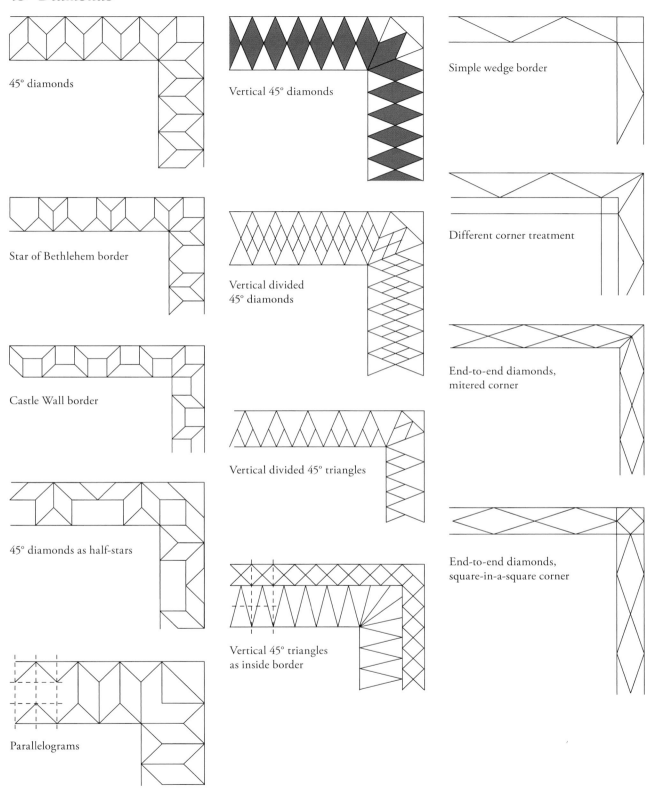

45° diamonds

Star of Bethlehem border

Castle Wall border

45° diamonds as half-stars

Parallelograms

Vertical 45° diamonds

Vertical divided
45° diamonds

Vertical divided 45° triangles

Vertical 45° triangles
as inside border

Simple wedge border

Different corner treatment

End-to-end diamonds,
mitered corner

End-to-end diamonds,
square-in-a-square corner

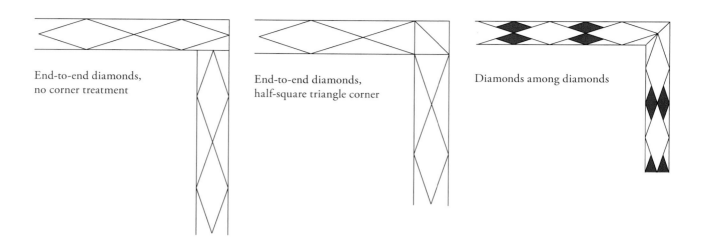

End-to-end diamonds, no corner treatment

End-to-end diamonds, half-square triangle corner

Diamonds among diamonds

# Log Cabin Borders

The use of Log Cabin blocks in borders makes a great outside or inside frame.

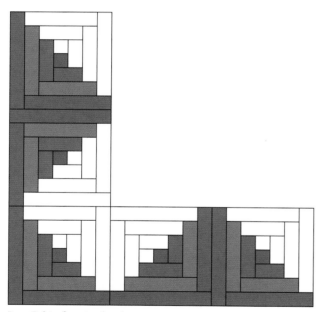

Log Cabin framing border

Log Cabin zigzag border

# Jazzy New-Style Borders

We have included a few more modern-looking borders to jazz up your quilts.

Gallery of modern-style borders

# Batting and Backing

Photo by C&T Publishing

# CHOOSING BATTING FOR YOUR NEW QUILTS

One of the most overlooked, least understood, and least discussed products in quiltmaking is batting. This key ingredient can either enhance a quilt's beauty or detract from and distort the quilt's surface. No one batting is appropriate for every quilt. Quilters must consider factors such as desired surface texture, weight, warmth, loft, drape, shrinkage, fiber content, washability, bearding properties, ease of needling, and so forth. All of these factors play as important a role in a quilt's overall appearance as do fabric choices, design piecing, and appliqué techniques. Remember, a top is not a quilt until it is quilted, and batting makes a top a quilt.

Machine quilting adds another dimension to your batting choices. As a beginner, you want to use a batting that will cooperate with you and your machine to eliminate distortion and thus frustration. As your skills improve, so will your willingness to take on more unruly battings and larger quilts. The fiber content, manufacturing process, and loft of each different batting will affect the manageability and success of the quilting process.

There are many excellent battings on the market, but there is no one perfect batt. If you feel very confused by all the different battings available, don't feel alone, as most of us have a hard time keeping up with all the new products that continually appear. At the time of this writing, there are over 110 different battings on the market. Many of them are actually the same batting from the same factory with a different brand name on the package; but nonetheless, you have to sift through an awful lot of product to discover what is truly appropriate for your new quilt top. Unfortunately, most quilters have access to only a handful of different types and brands.

Harriet has heard for years that machine quilting makes the quilt stiff, or that the nylon thread used by many machine quilters causes this problem, when actually it is the batting and how it is finished. If you have a heavily needle-punched batting, it will obviously be stiffer when quilted than an open, delicate batting. Today's quilters have been sold on the softness of the batting and the ability to quilt 6″ or more apart, not on softness in the finished quilt. We see people pet batting, thinking the softer the fiber feels, the softer the quilt will be. Think about it—you will never pet the batting again once it is in between two layers of cotton fabric, so how can the tactile feel of the fiber really make a difference? Instead of petting batting, examine how the batting is made. If it is like a blanket, the quilt will be flatter, stiffer, and not very warm. If the batting is lightweight, loose in fiber, possibly even able to be torn, and a bit puffy, the quilt will finish to be softer, more pliable, and warmer. Warmth is retained from heat being caught in the loft of the fibers—dead air space. That is why polyester and wool are warm—not only because of the fiber, but because the batts are thicker (not heavier). The more you quilt on these two battings and flatten them out, the less warm they will be as quilts.

The fiber content of the batting will affect the look and feel of any quilt. Cotton, polyester, and wool are the most common batting fibers. There is a trend today, however, to create boutique battings—battings made from trendy fibers like corn, bamboo, soy, and believe it or not, "green" recycled plastic! When asked why these products are being put on the market, the answer Harriet has received is "because we can." Do you really want to sleep under a plastic quilt? And we thought polyester was hot! Bamboo is broken down the same way wood pulp is to produce the fiber, thereby making it exactly like rayon. There are few environmental benefits to the harsh chemicals used in this process, making it not such an earth-friendly product. Corn and soy are food sources, so do we really need to be taking those products and making batting? Trends are one thing, but the added expense of the products is not justified by what they don't deliver. Cotton, wool, polyester, and silk are every bit as good and have certainly stood the test of time in hundreds of years of quiltmaking history. As you start to investigate batting brands and fibers, don't get caught up in the latest marketing scheme. Keep to the look and feel of the end product to make your final decisions.

Terminology can get rather confusing as we talk about different types of battings, so we are adding a short list of definitions to clear things up a bit.

**Bearding**   This refers to the migration of fibers through the quilt top or backing fabric. Don't confuse bearding with puncture marks. Puncture marks occur when a dull or too-large needle pushes the batting fibers through the backing fabric in the needle hole. Hand quilters can also experience this with some battings if they use a rough thread or too much beeswax on the thread. The fibers of the batting can be dragged through the needle hole on the thread. True bearding will look a bit like shedding. Polyester is the biggest culprit, and the fibers will migrate to each other, causing pills to form on the top of the fabric. Wool can beard slightly, but after a couple of washings, this usually stops, as the fibers intermingle with one another because of the barbs on the fibers themselves. Cotton breaks off at the surface of the fabric and seldom if ever has a problem with bearding. Low-thread-count fabrics are also a big problem with polyester and wool battings.

**Bonding**   Bonding is the process that is used to hold batting fibers together to prevent fibers from shifting and migrating. Two different processes are used:

• *Thermal*   Low-melt polyester fibers are combined with wool, polyester, or cotton fibers and heated by means of an oven, radiant heat, or an ultrasonic wave. The temperature is high enough to melt the low-melt fibers but not the other fibers in the batting. When the fibers melt, they cling to the other fibers, causing bonding points.

• *Resin*   A light coating of resin or glaze is sprayed on both sides of the fiber web. It is then heated in an oven to dry and cure the batting. Resin-bonded battings generally have a higher, lighter loft that is easier to quilt through.

**Carding**   This process takes the fiber from the bale and turns it into a web. A rotating drum with barbs on its surface separates and combs the fibers into a web. This web can be used without any further treatment. Early cotton quilt battings were webs of carded cotton placed between two pieces of paper. The batts needed to be quilted ¼"–½" apart to prevent the fibers from shifting. The quilts that used these batts were very soft. Today the web is then either cross-lapped, needle-punched, bonded, or any combination of the three.

**Loft**   The thickness of the batting is referred to as *loft*. It can also refer to the resilience of the fibers over a period of time.

**Needle-punching**   This mechanical process uses boards of embedded barbed needles that intermingle the fibers. As the batting web moves down the line, the needle boards pierce the layers and interlock the fibers into a fairly tight product. This is felting, or the making of a nonwoven fabric. The more needles or the slower the batting passes through the machine, the more tight and heavy the needling is. You will see various weights and thicknesses of these battings on the market.

**Scrim**   This is a very thin, sheer layer of polypropylene, similar to a lightweight interfacing. It is an added layer to the batting web that is then needle-punched to one or both sides of the batting. Scrim lets you quilt farther apart but can have a hard and fairly stiff surface. Battings with scrim are not the best choice for bed quilts but do work well for craft products like place mats, table runners, jackets, and so forth.

# Traditional Cotton Quilt Battings

The most commonly used natural fiber in quiltmaking is cotton. As evidenced by antique quilts, cotton stands the test of time. Whether you desire a batting that reacts like those products available in the 1800s or 1930s, or you want the more contemporary look of the new products, both are available. Vintage-style cotton batts require closer quilting (1″ and closer) and will have a higher percentage of shrinkage than the newer needle-punched batts that can be quilted up to 3″ apart. Claims are made that if a scrim binder is added, you can quilt up to 8″–10″ apart!

Cotton is still king in the batting market. More battings are made using cotton than any other fiber. Here are some of the characteristics of cotton that accommodate the needs of today's machine quilters.

- The cotton fibers of the batting stick to the quilt top and backing fabrics, preventing the shifting, slipping, distortion, and stretching that occur with polyester battings under the machine. This allows us to pin baste less, and eliminates puckers, tucks, and ruffled borders on our machine-quilted quilts.

This is the major reason for a beginning machine quilter to use cotton battings.

- Because the fibers do stick together and the batting is much thinner, when the quilt is rolled to go through the sewing machine, the roll is much smaller.

- Most cotton battings shrink some when washed. The shrinkage is generally at the same rate or higher than that of the cotton fabrics used in the quilt top. Shrinkage can be beneficial for several reasons:

a. It gives the quilt an aged look, which is desirable when trying to replicate an antique quilt.

b. When you are just learning to machine quilt, there are glitches in your work that you want to camouflage.

The shrinkage of the batting, when the quilt is first laundered, causes puckering around the stitching. This makes it difficult to tell how the quilt was quilted and hides many of the little problem areas. This helps you learn faster, as you can quilt on real quilt tops instead of spending hours practicing on muslin.

- Cotton is extremely comfortable to sleep under. Cotton breathes, allowing excess heat to escape. It makes excellent baby quilts.

- Cotton endures. Even with hard use, cotton ages gracefully, becoming softer and cuddlier with age.

- Pure cotton battings do not beard.

Photo by C&T Publishing

# Needle-Punched Cotton Battings

Needle-punched cotton batting became available as a craft batting in the early 1990s. It was intended for wall quilts and craft products but soon became a staple for quilts because of the 6″–10″ distance between quilting lines that was advertised. The first of these products had a scrim binder added during the felting process. This seemed very appealing to quilters who didn't want to quilt the traditional cotton battings that required 1″ or closer stitching. Many brands are now available, often the same product in different packaging produced at the same factory for different batting companies. Much like fabric production, one factory will make the same product—with a few minor differences—to be sold by several different private labels.

The softest and most drapable of the needle-punched battings are the ones without a scrim binder. They can be a bit more fragile and stretchy and might not be the best choice for wallhangings. We suggest that none of these battings without scrim be quilted farther apart than 3″, although the packaging will state 4″–6″. The more the quilt is quilted, the more durable it is. This is where these battings fall into trouble, as the more you quilt them, the flatter and stiffer they get. When selecting one of these battings, compare the amount of needle-punching and the denseness in several brands. Don't get caught up in the softness of the fiber. This has nothing to do with the end product!

> *Note* ❧ Many batting brands suggest that they can be quilted up to 10″ apart. We would like you to be aware of a basic problem with this misleading claim. What is being said is that the batting will not fall apart if quilted up to 10″ apart. However, those making the claim are not taking into consideration the weight and the wear and tear on the limited number of quilting stitches that are expected to hold everything together. Quilts are heavy, and even heavier when wet during washing and drying. When a quilt is quilted farther apart than 3″, there are not enough quilting lines to support this weight. This causes broken stitches and quilts that wear quickly and look less than healthy in a very short period of time. We would like you to consider keeping your quilting lines no farther apart than 3″ when planning your quilting design. If you look at the beautiful antique quilts that have survived for the past 150-plus years, you'll notice that they are heavily quilted, especially compared with many of the quilts that have been produced in the last 20 years of quiltmaking. If you want your labor of love to last through years and years of use, try to avoid the temptation of taking the easy way out and doing minimal quilting on your tops. With good batting choices and adequate quilting, your quilts should look lovely for a long, long time.

Photo by C&T Publishing

# Cotton/Polyester Blends

Fairfield started blending polyester with cotton in 1979, and by the 1990s, blending became quite the trend. Blending fibers together can give the advantages of both fibers in the product. The polyester and cotton blends are some of today's most popular battings. The polyester adds a bit of loft to the cotton, making it lighter and easier to hand quilt, as well as warmer. The most common blend proportion is 80% cotton and 20% polyester. You will see, however, a variety of proportions, and this can account for a vast difference in the behavior and feel of the batting after it is quilted.

Photo by C&T Publishing

# Miscellaneous Blends of Different Fibers

The latest trend in battings is to blend unique fibers together to get various results. We call these boutique battings, as they are generally hard to find, and the price is usually quite a bit higher than cotton and cotton/polyester blend battings. Many of these battings feel and look just like 100% cotton battings once quilted. Make sure you see and feel a quilted sample, or make one of your own before investing the higher price for these battings. You might be just as happy with a tried and true cotton batting that has been around for a long time.

Photos by C&T Publishing

# 100% Wool

Harriet worked with Hobbs Bonded Fibers in the 1990s to bring out the first machine-washable quilt batting made of 100% wool. You might ask—why wool? Wool is the fiber of choice when warmth and durability are needed, and we now use it as a substitute for polyester when natural fibers are desirable. The comfort of wool is universally recognized as superior to man-made (plastic) fibers. It is warm and lofty without being heavy, but can be quilted extremely close without getting stiff and hard. Wool quilts are a cut above most others.

Wool has characteristics that no other fiber provides. First, the wool fiber has built-in crimp, giving it bounce and loft that allows it to always return to its original shape. Wool has a recovery rate from compression of 95%, which is better than any other fiber. (Polyester averages 73%, depending on the type of polyester fiber treatment used.) This resiliency provides long-lasting beauty and warmth.

Wool batting provides superb insulation. The interlocking fibers breathe, allowing excess heat to disperse from the body. This allows our skin to remain warm yet dry. It moderates temperature, so you never get too hot or too cold when sleeping under it. Wool gives warmth without weight. It is naturally hygroscopic and can absorb up to 33% of its own weight in moisture without feeling damp, as opposed to 4% for synthetics and 8% for cotton. This makes it a perfect quilt for a damp, cold climate. Polyester tends to become clammy when damp.

Wool is naturally flame-resistant. When exposed to flames, it smolders at a low temperature and self-extinguishes with a cool ash, making it an extremely safe fiber to use for small children.

A concern many have concerning wool is mildew and insect damage. When it is between two layers of cotton fabric—the top and the backing—wool does well. Moths do not eat cotton, so they cannot get to the wool if it is totally covered. In addition, moths do not eat wool fibers unless dirt—their food—is attached to the fibers. The

Photo by C&T Publishing

fibers are damaged as the moth eats the dirt. You can protect your quilts, as well as any other wool items, by keeping them clean.

High-quality wool battings are made from preshrunk fibers. This keeps the fibers from shrinking when the quilt is washed. There will be a slight shrinkage amount in all wool battings. Be sure to dry your quilt in the dryer until just damp dry, then remove it and lay it out flat to dry. Drying your quilt bone dry will cause the fibers to shrink, and it will take some time for them to relax and lie flat again. Laying the quilt out flat just before it is completely dry, when the fibers are still relaxed, lets the quilt retain its soft loft.

# THE BATTING TEST

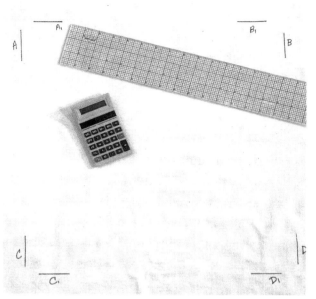

Photo by Sharon Risedorph

Now you probably feel totally confused and overwhelmed by the number of different battings available—and we didn't cover them all! Don't feel alone, as most of us have a hard time keeping up with all the new products that continually appear. Remember, confusion is the beginning of knowledge! We suggest that you obtain samples of, and thoroughly test, every batting you can get a piece of and every new batting product that appears on the market. If you will take the time to do the tests below, you will know everything you need to make your quilts have the exact look you want, and you will know how they will age, how close you need to quilt them, and so forth. You truly have no valid excuse not to do these tests if you want to be a true quilt-maker. The information you glean from them is invaluable.

First, collect three 14″ squares of every batting you can find.

**Note** 🌿 Please do not prewash any batting. Battings are not stable enough to withstand being wet, then dried. Uneven shrinkage, tearing, and stretching are a few of the problems you will encounter if you try to wash a batting. If shrinkage is a concern, after the samples are completed, you will be able to see the look of the batting after it is quilted, washed, and dried.

Next, create a pile of 14″ squares of high-quality muslin (quilt-shop quality only) that is prewashed and a pile that is unwashed. Label the squares with a permanent marker to identify those washed and unwashed. In the center of each of these squares, draw a perfect 6″ square with a permanent marker. These squares will be the tops of the blocks.

For the backing squares, sew a 7¼″ strip of black cotton to a 7¼″ strip of muslin. Cut into 14″ squares. You will need a pile of these made from preshrunk fabric *and* a pile from unwashed fabric.

You are now ready to layer the batting and fabric together. Do so in the following order:

**1.** One piece of batting with unwashed fabric—top and back.

**2.** One piece of the same batting with prewashed fabric—top and back.

Label the muslin square with the following information: the brand of batting, whether the fabric is prewashed or not, and any other information you feel is pertinent—like when the batting was purchased.

You should have one square of the batting being tested left. Make a copy of the Batting Sample Test Sheet (page 100) for every brand and type of batting you are testing, and staple the remaining batting square to it. Use it as a control sample for future comparison against new batts of the same brand to compare for consistency.

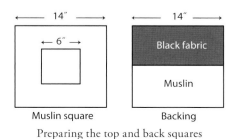

Preparing the top and back squares

If you find that the batting looks and feels different from the one you tested, you may want to run a new test on the new batt to see if it will perform differently from the original.

Now you will need to quilt the samples. If you are a hand quilter as well as a machine quilter, hand quilt half of the block and machine quilt the other half. On the form, make a note of whether you enjoyed quilting this batting and which method you preferred. If you are not a hand quilter, simply machine quilt the entire block. Quilt within the distances that are given on the package, or to your liking, but never quilting farther apart than 3″.

This is an excellent time to experiment with various threads and needles. The rayon, metallic, and cotton embroidery threads will react differently to different battings. Work out the machine tension settings and problems here, instead of on your quilt. Also experiment with the various needles available to see which type and size give you the best results on your machine. Use these batting samples to learn as much as possible. Also, note any tension adjustments that were needed for that particular batting, or differences in tension setting for various types and brands of threads and needles. Stitch length settings and preferences can also be noted for each batting.

Once you've quilted the sample, measure the 6″ square. Using those measurements in the following formula, compute to see if you have lost any size from quilting (a process known as *contraction*). Many battings will cause a size loss in the finished size of the quilt simply from the take-up that occurs in the quilting process.

% of shrinkage = (original − final) ÷ (original × 100)

Make a note of any size changes. Finish the edges by serging or zigzag stitching.

Once you have done this, it is time to wash and dry the quilt blocks. Wash and dry them the way you would care for your finished quilts. Once the blocks have dried, organize them so that the samples of the same brand of batting are together. Look at them and start to form your own opinions. Is one sample too wrinkled and another too flat? Do you really like the sample with the unwashed fabric and unwashed batting, but the pre-washed fabric and unwashed batting did not work out too well? Start to eliminate the combinations that distort the blocks or just don't appeal to you. Be aware of your feelings toward the look of the sample. You will find that you may like one combination, but your best friend prefers another. This is okay. Quilting is a very personal skill, and we should be making quilts that appeal to us and look like what we like, not just trying to please everyone else. If you like the finished result—go for it! It's your quilt.

Next, remeasure the 6″ square in the center of each block and rework the shrinkage formula. This gives you the total amount of size loss due to contraction and due to shrinkage from washing and drying. Now you can use these findings to determine if you need to make your quilt top a bit larger than the finished quilt needs to be, based on how the batting performs. Shrinkage doesn't need to be feared; learn about it instead and make it work for you.

The reason for the black on the back is to help look for bearding problems. Are tiny fibers migrating to the surface of the fabric? Are many fibers migrating? If so, this batting would not be a good choice for dark fabrics. Also, look at the top of the block. Is the dark color shadowing through the batting to the top of the block and discoloring (in appearance only) the top surface? This is a typical problem with polyester batting. It also dilutes the color of light-colored fabrics, making them appear slightly gray or tired looking. Cotton battings are opaque, and light cannot pass through them. You will not see the color coming from the back to the top on a cotton batt because of this. The cotton also keeps the true color in the top fabric by providing a layer that light cannot penetrate to dilute. If you want to put a dark backing on a light quilt top, you can if you are wise in your batting choice.

Once you have filled out the form, wash and dry all the samples again. Continue to do this week after week. Make a mark on each square every time it is washed and dried.

Examine the samples after 5 washings, again after 10 washings, and so forth. After 10 to 15 washings, see how the batting is holding up. Is this a batting you could use in a baby quilt and wash weekly, if not daily, and have it hold up? Alternatively, is it fragile and not aging well under such use? Determine where and when these battings would be appropriate in the quilts you make. Not all quilts lie on closet shelves, but not all quilts are on kids' beds either.

Now you have the start of a batting library. Before you start a new project, look through the batting samples before you buy the fabric and/or do anything with it. As you look through the samples, ask yourself these questions about your new quilt:

- Do I want natural fiber, synthetic, or a blended batting?

- Do I want it thick or thin?

- Do I want it flat or fluffy?

- Do I want to hand quilt it or machine quilt it?

- How close do I want to quilt this quilt?

- Do I need this quilt for warmth, or do I want a cooler quilt—is it for summer, spring, fall, or winter temperatures?

- Is the quilt going to be washed a lot, or is it just for show?

- Is the quilt going to hang on the wall or lie on a bed?

- Do I need the quilt to look antique or contemporary— should it be smooth or puckered?

If you can answer all these questions for every quilt you make, you will be matching the appropriate batting to every quilt top you make. This information is not available in a quilt book or classroom. The only way to truly learn about batting is to do the samples. We know that most of you won't do the samples. You will probably say that you don't have time to waste on muslin samples. However, you do have the time and money to invest in a quilt top that you love, only to be disappointed in the results because the batting does not look right.

Think about it this way—as you get further into the art of quilting and start practicing various machine-quilting techniques, you will need samples to practice on. What if you were to spend some time to collect the ingredients and layer them together as suggested above? Then when you sit down to practice your quilting skills, you already have the practice pieces ready. Instead of throwing away your practice blocks, you set them aside to test. As you practice, you are not wasting an hour of time, an ounce of batting, or a yard of fabric. You are learning to quilt, and you are developing an invaluable reference library of brands and types of battings, as well as what combinations they can be successfully used in and how well they wear with repeated launderings. What else could you ask from just a few hours of preparation and practice?

# Batting Sample Test Sheet

Brand name: _____

Fiber content: _____

Sizes available: _____

Recommended quilting distance: _____

How did it needle? _____

    Hand: _____

    Machine: _____

Thread used: _____

    Top: _____

    Bobbin: _____

Needle used: _____

Appearance after quilting: _____

_____

Bearding? _____

Shadowing through? _____

Contraction when quilted? _____

Shrinkage after washing? _____

*Opinion of appearance after washing:* _____

_____

Which combination did I like best? _____

_____

Appearance after 5 washings: _____

    after 10 washings: _____

    after 15 washings: _____

Quilts I have used this batting in: _____

_____

Other comments: _____

_____

_____

# SPLICING BATTING

Battings come in many sizes, but often you need a larger size than is available in a particular brand, or you want to use up large pieces of the same product that you have left over from other projects. This is when you will need to splice two batting pieces together. It is common to butt two straight edges and whipstitch them together. The problem with this method is that the splice will appear as a "break line" through the quilt, especially as the quilt ages. Harriet suggests overlapping the two pieces of batting by 6″–8″. Cut a serpentine line through both layers. The gradual undulating curves will butt together perfectly once the end of each layer is removed.

Hand stitch the batting together using ½″-long loose herringbone stitches. This serpentine-stitched splice will eliminate any unsightly evidence of where you joined the pieces.

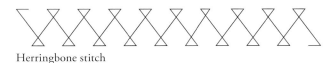

Herringbone stitch

6″–8″ overlap

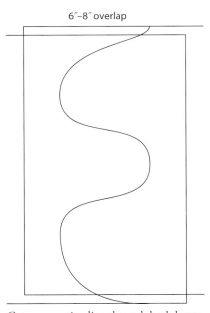

Cut a serpentine line through both layers.

# QUILT BACKING

When choosing a backing (also known as a lining) for your quilt, think about letting it complement the front. It used to be that most backings were solids or muslin, but many backings are now made from prints or even pieced units.

If you're an excellent quilter, a solid fabric will really show off your quilting. However, if you're new to quilting, a print will camouflage any uneven stitches or contrasting threads.

The backing fabric must be the same fiber content, quality of cloth, weight, and thread count as the fabrics used for the top. Although a limited number of prints, as well as muslin, are available in 90″ widths or wider for backings, the majority of fabrics used for backings are 45″ wide.

## Determining Yardage

To determine the yardage needed for backing, be sure to add 2″ to 3″ to the size of the quilt top on all four sides. It helps to make a sketch of the quilt top measurements in order to determine what seams might be needed, and whether to make them horizontal or vertical for the best use of the yardage. The illustration (at right) shows various seam configurations to use in calculations. When figuring yardage, don't forget to subtract the width of the selvages, as they need to be removed before you piece the lengths together. The standard width used to figure yardage is 42″.

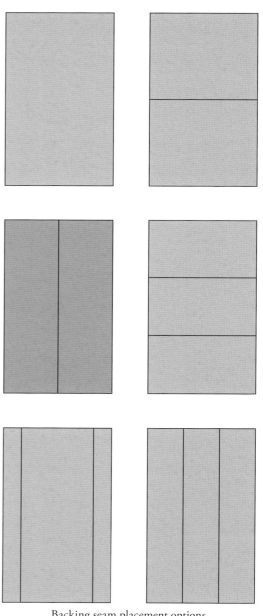

Backing seam placement options

Following are backing yardage guidelines for various quilt sizes.

**Quilt tops** 40″ wide or *narrower* require only 1 quilt length of fabric (plus 4″ to 5″) because the fabric is wide enough to accommodate the width of the quilt top.

**Quilt tops** 40″ wide or *wider* require 2 pieces of fabric seamed together. If you buy 2 lengths of fabric to back a quilt 60″ long, you need 3½ yards ([64″ × 2] ÷ 36″ = 3.56, or 3½ yards). If the quilt is 44″ wide, and the seams will run horizontally, you would need only 2⅔ yards ([48″ × 2] ÷ 36″ = 2.67 = 2⅔ yards). Quite a saving! In this case, horizontal seams utilize the width of the fabric with the least left over.

**Twin and throw-size quilts** are generally around 72″ wide or square. Using the *Tip:* Yardage Formula (at right), we find that 2 quilt widths of fabric are needed. If the quilt is 72″ × 90″ and the seams are vertical, we need 5¼ yards. Horizontal seams would require 3 widths, requiring 6 yards. Therefore, vertical seams would be the best choice.

**Full-size quilts** average 81″ × 96″ finished. Again, 2 quilt widths will just be wide enough, requiring 5⅓ yards. Horizontal seams would require 8 yards.

**Queen-size quilts** average 90″ × 108″ finished. For vertical seams, 3 quilt widths of fabric (about 9½ yards) are required, but only 8 yards for horizontal seams.

*Note:* If you choose to use vertical seams, they appear the most balanced if you keep a full width in the center. Divide the remaining width equally between the remaining 2 lengths, and sew them on either side of the center panel.

**King-size quilts** are generally 120″ × 120″. A full 3 quilt widths, each 3½ yards long—a total of 10½ yards—are needed for the backing, regardless of which direction the seams run, as the quilt is square.

These yardages are just examples based on the specific quilt sizes given. It is easy to figure backing yardage if you simply plug your quilt top size into the yardage formula.

---

### Tip ✳ Yardage Formula

An easy formula for yardage calculation is as follows:

Quilt top width ÷ fabric width (minus selvages) = number of quilt lengths of backing needed (round up to the nearest whole number)

Then:

Quilt top length (in inches) × number of lengths needed ÷ 36″ = number of yards to buy

---

We recommended that you lightly starch your unwashed backing fabric before using it. If you prewash the fabric, starching it is strongly recommended.

# Binding

# PREPARING THE QUILT FOR BINDING

Once the layers have been quilted, you are ready to prepare the edges for binding. You will need to first remove the excess batting and backing from the edges, square the corners, and straighten the edges.

There are two schools of thought about preparing to bind a quilt. Some quilters leave the batting and backing in place until the binding has been attached, then trim the excess away. We prefer the more traditional method of trimming the edges of all three layers, then applying the binding. Try both, and choose the one you prefer and get the best results from.

## Squaring Up the Quilt Top

**1.** To trim the edges, use a long, wide ruler and a large square ruler. Starting in a corner, use the square ruler to check for squareness, and trim the edges. Be sure that you align the ruler lines with the seamlines within the body of the quilt.

*Note* 🌿 This photo shows trimming off extra width that was added to the final border size.

Aligning ruler lines with seamlines in quilt

**2.** Trim the sides, keeping the border width accurate and aligning with the corner cuts. Repeat this for all 4 sides.

**3.** Fold the quilt ends into the center to make sure that all the widths are the same. Repeat for the sides.

**4.** If the quilting runs right up to the raw edge, you won't have to add additional stabilization. If the edges are loose, we suggest that you machine baste the edges together (using long stitches) to eliminate the possibility of distortion when sewing on the binding. *Note:* When basting by machine, be very careful not to stretch the edges as they pass under the foot. A walking foot is a great help in this process.

The quilt top has been pieced, layered, and quilted. All that now remains is to close up the edges, and at long last, your quilt will be finished, ready to wash and use. It is an exciting step ahead, and one you must not rush through. It's important that the binding look as nice as the rest of the quilt. If the binding is sloppy and poorly attached and finished, it detracts from the whole quilt. Your finish work is critical to the look of the finished product.

When binding a straight-edged quilt, we prefer straight-grain binding over bias binding, as it keeps the quilt edge straight with no ripples. A bias binding is stretchy and may give the quilt a "stretched" appearance along the edge. In addition, the quilt may appear to ripple when hung or placed on a bed. However, a bias binding is recommended for a quilt with rounded corners and scallops.

One argument for bias binding is that the edge of the binding will not wear as badly because there is not a single thread in the weave that runs along the edge (as there is in straight-grain binding). Our argument is for crosswise-cut binding strips, but cut slightly off-grain. Most of the time the grain is off on the bolt. Therefore, when you fold the center fold to the selvages, the strips are not perfectly on grain, yet they are not true bias. Instead of straightening the grain, leave it off-grain, and cut the strips perpendicular to the center fold (on the crosswise grain). This gives you the best of both methods; the grain is slightly off, allowing more threads to take the wear, but it is not nearly as stretchy as bias.

## Straight-Grain Double-Fold Binding

There are several different options for preparing binding, but for now, we will address the easiest—straight-grain double-fold binding.

Double-fold binding is made from strips cut from 1¼″ to 2¼″ wide and folded in half. This is also known as *French-fold binding*. The width of the strip depends on the thickness of the batting used and how wide you want the finished binding to be. If you're reproducing a quilt from the 1800s, you'll want your binding to be as narrow as you can possibly work with—generally ¼″ wide or narrower, finished—for authenticity. These strips would be cut 1¼″ to 1½″ wide and sewn on with an ⅛″ seam allowance.

A really nice-looking binding for most quilts is about ⅜″ finished, using 2″ cut strips doubled and a scant ¼″ seam allowance. Regardless of the width of binding you choose, remember that once it's wrapped around the edge of the quilt, it should not be empty, but filled completely with the batting and quilt layers.

### Cutting Binding Strips

Cut binding strips 4 times the desired finished width plus ½″ (or as indicated in the chart below) for seam allowances and ⅛″–¼″ to go around the thickness of the batting. The fatter the batting, the more you need to add here.

| | |
|---|---|
| ³⁄₁₆″ binding = 1¼″ cut | ⅛″ seam allowance |
| ¼″ binding = 1½″ cut | ³⁄₁₆″ seam allowance |
| ⁵⁄₁₆″ binding = 1¾″ cut | scant ¼″ seam allowance |
| ⅜″ binding = 2″ cut | ¼″ seam allowance |
| ½″ binding = 2¼″ cut | generous ¼″ seam allowance |

To determine how much binding you need, calculate the perimeter (distance around your quilt). Figure 2 × the length + 2 × the width = the minimum inches of binding needed. For example, a quilt 60″ × 80″ would require 280″ of binding.

We recommend that you add a minimum of 12″ to this sum to allow for turning corners, piecing strips together, and joining the ends together on the quilt. So how many strips is this? If you do the figuring based on 42″ strips (selvage to selvage), then 292″ ÷ 42″ = 6.95 strips needed. Round up to 7 strips across the width of the fabric, and multiply by the cut width of the strip. This is how much yardage is needed.

The chart below gives you an estimate of the yardage needed to bind various sizes of quilts with straight-grain binding. These measurements are based on a ½″ finished binding.

| Estimated Yardage for ½″-Wide Straight-Grain Binding | | | |
|---|---|---|---|
| Quilt size | # of 2¼″-wide strips | Inches of fabric | Yards of fabric |
| Wallhanging (36″ × 36″) | 4 | 9 | ¼ |
| Twin (54″ × 90″) | 7 | 16 | ½ |
| Double (72″ × 90″) | 8 | 18 | ½ |
| Queen (90″ × 108″) | 10 | 22½ | ⅝ |
| King (120″ × 120″) | 12 | 27 | ¾ |

## Joining Straight-Grain Strips

### Method A: Joining the Strips Together

The strips need to be joined with a 45°-angle seam.

**1.** Keeping the strips double (wrong side to wrong side), position the 45° angle of the ruler on the edge of the strip as shown, then cut. Repeat with the remainder of the strips.

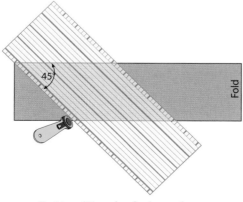

Position 45° angle of ruler, and cut.

**2.** To join the strips together, line up the edges, offsetting by ¼″, and sew with a ¼″ seam allowance.

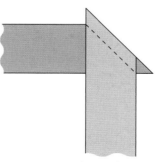

Join strip ends together.

**3.** Continue joining all the strips together into a continuous length. Press the seams open.

## Method B: Joining the Strips Together

Method A had you joining the binding strips using a 45° angle at both ends of each strip. The strips were joined by chain sewing the ends into a continuous length. This alternative method will eliminate the need to cut the ends at 45° angles. Instead, make sure that the ends are perfectly squared off.

Position the strips at 90° angles to one another. Stitch from corner to corner, keeping the triangle of the corner on the right side of the needle when stitching. Use a stitch length of 1½ or 2.

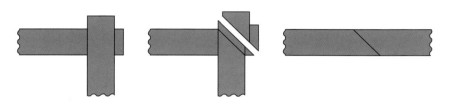

Sewing from corner to corner

Open the strip to check for accuracy. The edges of the strips should be perfectly straight on both sides of the seam. Trim the seam allowance to ¼" and press the seam open.

# Bias Binding

We find that when we are manipulating binding around tight inside and outside corners, bias binding is more pliable and easier to work with. You might want to make a sample to determine the width of binding you desire on your chosen project. As you have read, we use a narrower binding than is the general rule. The reason for this is the thickness of the batting. Back in the 1980s when we used thick, fluffy polyester batting, the binding needed to be cut 2½" to accommodate the thickness of the batting and to cover the wider seam allowances that we sewed with then. Now that we sew with narrower seams and our batting is very thin, the binding needs to be cut narrower to give a good sharp edge and to have the binding completely full. If the binding doesn't cover the edge of the batting tightly, the edge will not wear well and will have a sloppy appearance.

| | | |
|---|---|---|
| **Wallhanging** (36" × 36") | 4 strips × 1¾" wide = 7" | ¼ yard |
| **Twin** (54" × 90") | 8 strips × 1¾" wide = 14" | ⅜ yard |
| **Full** (72" × 90") | 8 strips × 1¾" wide = 14" | ⅜ yard |
| **Queen** (90" × 108") | 10 strips × 1¾" wide = 18" | ½ yard |
| **King** (120" × 120") | 12 strips × 1¾" wide = 21" | ⅝ yard |

## Binding Widths

When making bias binding, the easiest way is to use the continuous method. The chart on the next page will help you determine how big to cut your square based on the amount of binding needed.

1. Cut a square of fabric the size needed. Cut the square in half diagonally, creating 2 triangles.

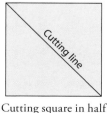

Cutting square in half diagonally

2. Sew these triangles together, as shown, with a ¼" seam.

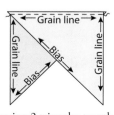

Sewing 2 triangles together

**3.** After sewing, open the triangles and press the seam open. This will give you a parallelogram. Using a ruler, mark the entire backside with lines spaced the width you need to cut your bias. Cut on the first line about 5″.

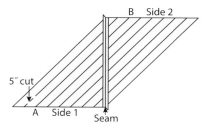

Press seam open, measure, and draw lines.

**4.** Connect A and B, and side 1 and side 2 to form a tube. (The cut edge on the first line will line up with the raw edge at B. This will allow the first line to be offset by a line). Pin the raw ends together, making sure that the lines match. Sew with a ¼″ seam allowance.

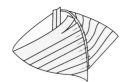

Offset by one line and sew tube.

If you have aligned the seam properly, you will have an extra strip at each end. Continue cutting on the line you started in Step 3. As you cut on the line, the tube will become one long, continuous piece of bias binding.

Once you have cut all the lines, press the binding in half and starch lightly. At the cutting mat, use your ruler to measure from the folded edge and trim the raw edges to create a very straight and accurate binding. This will give you a very straight finished binding.

Here is an easy formula for figuring the size square you need for the required length of bias: Divide the square size by the width of your bias and then multiply only the whole number of the answer by the square size again.

*Example:* A 22″ square divided by 1¾″ (width of cut bias) = 12.57. Multiply 12 by 22″ = 264″ of continuous bias yielded. If you need this in yardage, divide by 36.

Obviously, these yardages are for straight-sided quilts. If you are planning to bind the outside edges of hexagons or other uneven edges, you will need to actually measure how much binding is needed for each hexagon and multiply that by how many hexagons you will be binding. Be sure to add quite a bit of extra to allow for the many turns—both inside and out.

| | | | |
|---|---|---|---|
| **Wallhanging** | 36″ × 36″ + 12″ = 156″ | 18″ ÷ 1.75″ = 10 × 18″ = 180″ | 18″ square |
| **Twin** | 54″ × 90″ + 12″ = 300″ | 24″ ÷ 1.75″ = 13 × 24″ = 312″ | 24″ square |
| **Full** | 72″ × 90″ + 12″ = 336″ | 26″ ÷ 1.75″ = 14 × 26″ = 364″ | 26″ square |
| **Queen** | 90″ × 108″ + 12″ = 408″ | 28″ ÷ 1.75″ = 16 × 28″ = 448″ | 28″ square |
| **King** | 120″ × 120″ + 12″ = 492″ | 30″ ÷ 1.75″ = 17 × 30″ = 510″ | 30″ square |

Binding is a several-step process: You make your binding, stitch the binding to the quilt front, and then finish by stitching it to the back.

## Determining the Correct Seam Allowance for Applying Binding to a Quilt

Here is a clever way to determine the actual seam allowance needed for each size of binding:

1. Lay out the binding on the ironing board. Apply a light layer of heavy-duty starch to the wrong side of the binding. Fold the binding in half and press. The starch will help the layers stick together. Press the entire length of the binding strip.

> *Tip* ✳ For very accurate binding, use a ruler and rotary cutter to measure from the fold. Trim to be *exactly* the same width the entire length of the binding.

2. Fold the binding in thirds, but leave just a bit less than ⅛″ beyond the last fold on the raw-edge side. This extended edge is the allowance for the batting thickness.

3. Finger-press the folds. At your sewing machine, position the needle in the fold line of the first fold from the folded edge of the binding.

4. Position a barrier-type seam guide against the folded edge of the binding. This will be the seam allowance with which you will sew the binding onto the quilt.

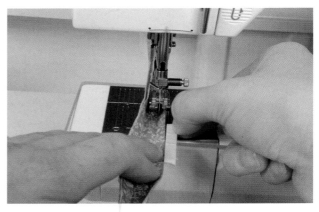

5. Sew a sample first. Start by stitching about 3″ of binding onto the quilt edge. Stop and wrap the binding. The folded edge should just cover the stitching on the back of the quilt. If it is too tight, take a slightly smaller seam; if it is a bit empty, take a slightly wider seam.

Following this method will give you perfect binding every time.

# Stitching the Binding to the Quilt Front: Method A

There are several ways to finish the ends when attaching binding. Here is the easiest.

**1.** Cut and join the strips using one of the two methods explained in Basic Binding: Two Methods (page 106). Starch the strips and press them in half lengthwise, wrong sides together. At one end of the strip, fold a ¼″ seam allowance over to the wrong side, and press. The point from the wrong side of the binding should be on the bottom, as shown in the illustration.

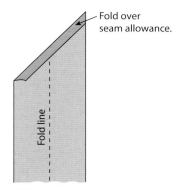

Fold ¼″ seam allowance on 45° angle.

**2.** With the long fold open, position the binding on top of the quilt top. Start stitching the binding at the point, stitching through only 1 thickness of the binding. Stitch for about 4″.

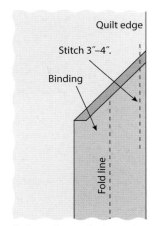

Stitch through one thickness from point.

**3.** Lift the presser foot and cut the threads. Fold the binding over to double. Start stitching about 1″ below the short edge of the point. Stitch the binding in place, aligning the edges exactly and stopping ¼″ from the corner.

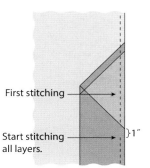

Fold binding over to double.

Stitch up to ¼″ (or your chosen seam allowance) from corner.

**4.** Turn the quilt so that you're lined up to sew the next side. Backstitch off edge. Fold the binding straight up toward the side you just sewed. Then refold toward the new edge, lining up the second fold with the outer edge of the quilt, and the raw edges of the binding with the raw edges of the quilt.

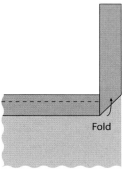

First fold for miter

**5.** Begin sewing at the outer edge of the quilt; sew through all the layers at the corner. Continue down the edge, repeating the corner treatment.

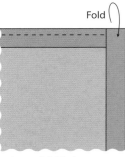

Second fold alignment

**6.** Once you've arrived back at the beginning, tuck the end of the binding into the pocket. Lower the needle into the fabric. Lay the end of the binding strip over the point and single thickness that was the starting point. Cut off the end just before the stitching that started going through all the layers. Tuck the end into the pocket, and finish closing the seam.

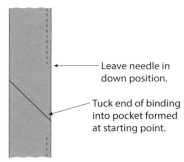

Leave needle in down position.

Tuck end of binding into pocket formed at starting point.

Tuck in end, and close stitching.

# Stitching the Binding to the Quilt Front: Method B

In Method A, we joined the ends of the binding on the quilt by sewing down the bottom point and stuffing the finishing end into the pocket created by the sewing at the start. This time, we are going to join the ends with a seam so that this join will look exactly like the seams that joined the strips together.

**1.** Starting in the middle of one side of the quilt, leave about 8″ of binding loose before beginning to stitch. Make sure to cut the beginning tail at a 45° angle. Align the raw edges of the quilt with the binding. Begin stitching the binding onto the quilt edge.

**2.** At the corner, stop ¼″ from both edges of the quilt.

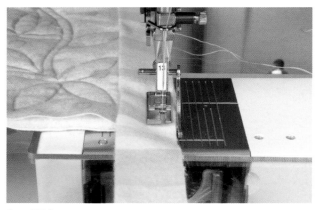

Stop ¼″ from corner.

*Tip* ✳ Check to see whether the bar in front of your needle on the presser foot measures ¼″ or whether there are markings on the side of the foot that measure ¼″. Many machines have this feature; this is an excellent way to know when to stop.

**3.** With the needle down, pivot the quilt and stitch straight backward off the edge of the binding.

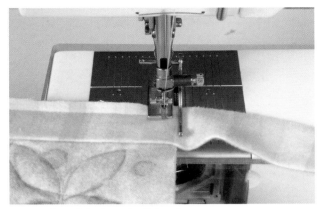

Pivot and stitch backward off the edge.

**4.** Pull the quilt out from under the foot a bit so that you can work with the corner. The mitered corner is a simple two-fold step. First, fold the free end of the binding over the stitched binding to form a 90° corner. The free end of the binding is off the quilt at this point. The diagonal fold in the corner of the binding will be the miter.

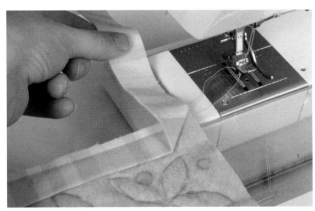

Fold binding back to start forming miter.

Second, fold the free end of the binding back onto the quilt. This second fold should line up with the top edge of the quilt. Make sure this fold is a couple of threads beyond the raw edge of the binding underneath.

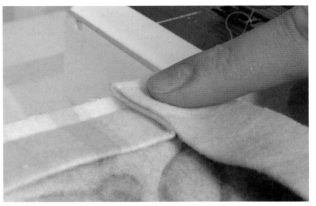

Bring binding over top to form miter.

**5.** Start stitching at the edge of the fold. Stitch the binding to this side of the quilt. Repeat for all the corners.

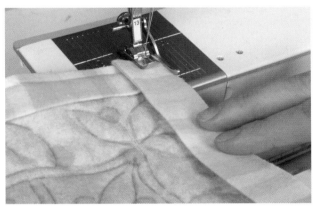

Start stitching at edge.

**6.** Once the binding has been attached all the way around the quilt, make sure you have left 12″–16″ open. On a flat surface and with the binding opened to a single thickness, pin the ending tail along the quilt edge.

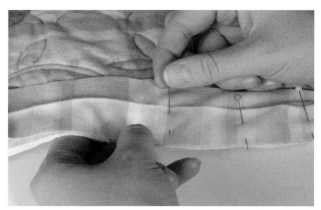

Pin end of binding flat to quilt layers.

**7.** Smooth the beginning tail over the ending tail. Following the cut edge of the beginning tail, draw a line on the ending tail with a removable marker. Check that this line is at a true 45° angle to the binding's long edges.

Beginning edge laid over flattened binding; mark.

**8.** Fold the beginning tail out of the way and add the seam allowance by drawing another line ½″ down from the first line. This second line is the cutting line, so make sure that you are marking and cutting to make the binding ½″ *longer* than the first line.

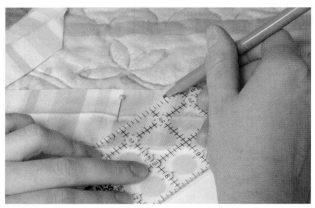

Add ½″ seam allowance.

**9.** Cut on the second line.

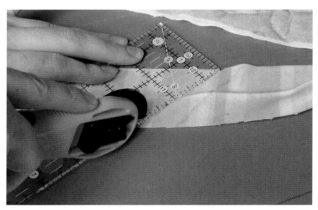

Cut.

**10.** Place the ends right sides together and join with a ¼″ seam allowance. Press the seam open. Press this section of binding in half and finish sewing to the edge of the quilt.

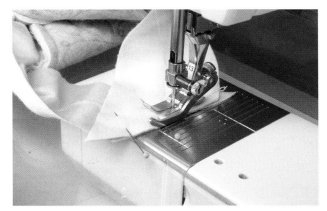

Join ends with ¼″ seam allowance.

# Final Sewing: Blind Stitch

If you blindstitch the binding by hand, we suggest that you use a 40-weight, three-ply hand quilting thread.

**1.** Wrap the binding around to the back of the quilt, placing the folded edge of the binding on top of the stitching line. You can either pin the binding in place, use binding clips to hold it, or glue it in place with Elmer's Washable School Glue. If using glue, apply a very small line, and press dry with the iron before hand stitching.

**2.** Begin the blind stitch by inserting the needle under the edge of the binding right at the fold edge of the binding. Next, put the needle into the quilt immediately across from where it is in the binding. You don't want to stitch through to the front—just into the batting. Let the needle travel approximately ¼″ through the inside of the quilt before emerging and traveling into the binding, again right at the edge. Continue in this manner.

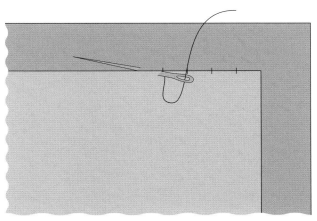

Finish edge with blind stitching.

**3.** When you reach the corners, you'll find that the corner (miter) is already formed on the top of the quilt, but you'll need to coax the miter on the back with your fingers. Fold one side down, then the other, creating a neat miter. The fold should be opposite that on the front side, with the bulk evenly distributed on both sides. This creates a flat corner.

# Final Sewing: Ladder Stitch

The ladder stitch is less visible than the blind stitch but is a bit slower.

Use a 40/3 quilting thread for strength and a size 9 or 10 sharp or appliqué needle. (Appliqué needles are more slender and longer than sharps.)

**1.** Knot your thread and then run the needle through a part of the seam allowance. Bring the needle into the fold of the binding. Go directly below this exit point of the needle into the batting and backing, just below the stitching line. Take a ¼″ stitch and pull the thread through the fabric.

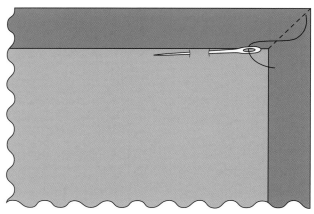

Stitch in batting and backing only.

**2.** Position the point of the needle directly above where it came out of the fabric and insert it into the fold of the binding. Take a ¼″ stitch and pull the thread through.

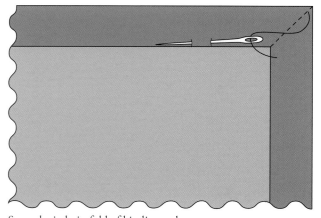

Second stitch, in fold of binding only.

**3.** The stitch is ¼″ in the fold, then ¼″ in the backing/batting, then ¼″ in the fold again. The stitches are straight down; there is no slant to them as with blind stitching.

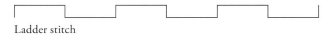

Ladder stitch

**4.** Repeat until you get to a corner. At the corner, stitch down each side of the miter with a very small stitch. Stitch to the end of the miter, push the needle through to the front side, and continue back down the front side of the miter. Once you get back to the inside corner, push the needle through to the back and continue down the binding with the longer stitch.

> *Tip* ✳ As you stitch, tighten the thread a bit every inch or so by pulling it gently. The stitches will disappear into the fabric.

# PRAIRIE POINTS

Prairie points are a fun way to add interest to the edge of a quilt. You can use many different scraps as with Method One or Two, or use only one or two colors if you use the continuous method. Choose the method that suits the look of the quilt.

Instead of a binding, this is an inserted edge finish. An inserted edge can include prairie points, scallops, ruffles, or piping. An inserted edge is attached to the front and the batting by sewing through both layers all the way around the quilt. The back is then folded over the seam allowance and blindstitched in place. Prairie points can be added after the quilt top is quilted—especially if the quilting extends to the edges of the quilt top—or even before the quilting is done.

## Method One

This is the traditional way of making points. It is accomplished by using small squares of fabric and folding them into triangles. These triangles are overlapped and sewn to the edge of the quilt in place of a binding.

To determine how many prairie points you need for each side of your quilt, use this formula. Take the length of your quilt, then divide by the finished base of a single prairie point, and multiply by 2 (for the overlap). For example, if you are making a 45″ × 60″ baby quilt, the length is 60″. If the triangle bases are 3″, then 60 ÷ 3 = 20 × 2 = 40 prairie points for each side of the quilt. The top and bottom edges are 45″. So 45 ÷ 3 = 15 × 2 = 30 points needed for the top and 30 for the bottom. You will need to make 140 prairie points for the quilt.

To determine how big a square to use for the size you want the finished prairie points to be, take the height of the finished point × 2 + ½″. That equals the size square to cut. If you want 2″ finished prairie points, you would use this formula:

2 × 2 = 4 + ½″ = 4½″ squares

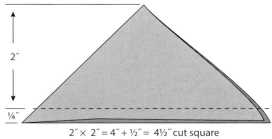

2″ × 2″ = 4″ + ½″ = 4½″ cut square

Figuring the size to start with

**1.** Fold each square in half diagonally, right side out. Fold in half again, forming a small triangle. Press.

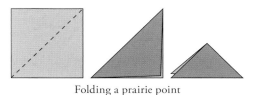

Folding a prairie point

**2.** Working from the quilt top front, align the long side of the folded triangle to the raw edge of the quilt top. The points will be facing in toward the quilt top. Begin at the center of one side of the quilt. Nest the points one inside the other, as shown below. Adjust the amount of overlap to fit the side of the quilt you are working on, and pin securely in place. At the corner, have the long edge of one prairie point start right on the raw edge. Stitch it onto the quilt top and batting.

Nesting points on edge of quilt top and batting

# Method Two

The second way to create prairie points for the edge of your quilt is to fold the square into a rectangle, wrong sides together. Press. Make 2 diagonal folds into the center to create a triangle that has a vertical line. Press it flat.

Folding square into rectangle

Overlap the prairie points on top of one another, as shown in the illustration. The points cannot nest with this method. Adjust the overlap along the edge of the quilt until the prairie points all fit evenly.

Overlapping points along edge of quilt

Prairie points are usually added after the quilting is completed. Trim the batting and backing to be even with the edge of the quilt top. Fold the backing away and pin it so that it cannot be caught when sewing the edge. Starting at one corner, sew the prairie points to the quilt top and batting, using a ¼″ seam allowance.

Sewing points to edge of quilt

Once you have sewn all four edges, trim out as much of the batting from this seam as possible. This will eliminate the bulk caused by the extra fabric from the triangles. Turn the prairie points so that they face out from the quilt top. The raw edge of the quilt top will be inside. Turn under ¼″ of the backing. Blindstitch the folded edge of the backing to the prairie point edges, completely covering the seam.

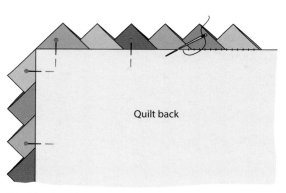

Stitching backing over seam

# Continuous-Band Points

A very slick way of making continuous-band prairie points has been floating around since before 1989, but the name of the inventor and its place of origin seem to have been lost. It has been in magazines, given out as free handouts by sewing machine companies, and offered in guild newsletters. Whoever came up with this great idea, we really appreciate it!

There are fewer possibilities for variation in color and fabrics with this method than with the individual squares, but it's certainly faster and easier. Because the prairie points are not made individually, they are always the same size and evenly spaced.

To determine the size of the strips for your prairie points, take your desired height of the prairie point plus ¼" × 4.

## One-Color Prairie Points

Our example here will produce an edging with triangles that finish to 1¾" high: 1.75 + .25 × 4 = 8". As always, we recommend that you make a sample to experience the technique and determine what your measurements will be.

**1.** Start by cutting an 8"-wide strip of fabric the same length as one edge of the quilt, plus about 6" extra. If necessary, piece strips together to get this needed length.

**2.** Place the wrong sides of the strips together and fold the strip in half lengthwise. Press well.

**3.** Place the fabric strip wrong side up, opened to the 8" width. Beginning at one end, start marking off 4" segments on one side of the band. On the opposite side, begin 2" in from the end and again mark off 4" segments. It makes no difference if one side is longer or has more squares than the other.

**4.** Cut the squares on the marked lines from the outer edge to the center pressed fold.

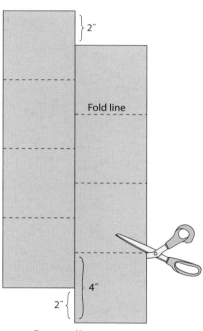

Prepare 4" segments on strip.

You will be pressing as you go, so work at the ironing board. Begin by turning the fabric wrong side up, and fold the points as follows:

**a.** Beginning with Point 1, place it nearest to you and make the first fold, as shown. Next, turn the top corner down for the second fold.

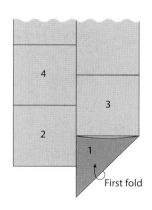

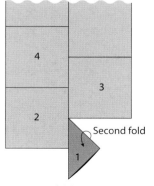

Begin folding process.

**b.** Move to Point 2 and make the first fold. Next, fold Point 1 across the bottom part of Point 2. Make the second fold of Point 2. This will enclose half of the base of Point 1. Pin in place.

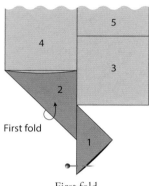

First fold

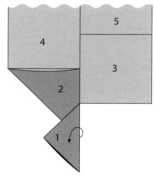

Fold Point 1 across bottom part of Point 2.

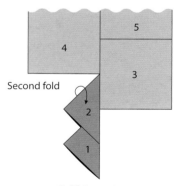

Fold Point 2.

**c.** Next, make the first fold of Point 3. Now fold Points 1 and 2 over and make the last fold on Point 3. This will enclose half of the base of Point 2. Pin in place.

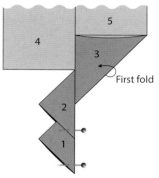

First fold of Point 3

**d.** Continue in this manner, alternating from side to side, until all the points are folded and pinned.

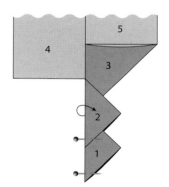

Fold Point 2 across bottom part of Point 3.

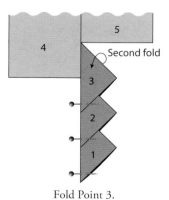

Fold Point 3.

**5.** Once the entire strip has been folded and pinned, machine stitch ⅛″ from the raw edge, removing pins as you go. Press.

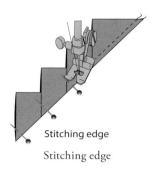

Stitching edge

Stitching edge

**6.** Repeat this process for each side of the quilt.

## Two-Color Prairie Points

Two-color prairie points are constructed the same as above but work with 2 strips, each a different color.

**1.** Start by cutting 2 strips, 1 each from different fabric. To determine how wide to cut them, use this formula: finished height × 2 + ¾". For this example, we want 2" finished points, so 2 × 2 + ¾" = 4¾".

**2.** Instead of folding a wide strip in half, you will be sewing the 2 different strips together, wrong sides together, with a ¼" seam. Press to the darker strip and starch lightly.

**3.** Lay the strip on the table with the seam allowance down and the wrong side up. Mark (4½" squares this time), cut, fold, and press as described for one-color prairie points.

**4.** Pin the prairie points in position on the right side of the quilt top, keeping the backing fabric out of the way. If there are any extra complete points beyond the edge of the quilt, cut them off. Do not cut through a point. Ease if necessary to make it fit the length of the edge.

**5.** Sew a ¼" seam allowance through all the layers except the backing. Trim any excess batting close to the stitching.

**6.** Once the prairie points have been sewn, fold them away from the quilt top and stitch the backing in place along the seamline on the back, using a blind stitch (page 115) or ladder stitch (page 116).

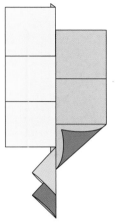

Working with two colors

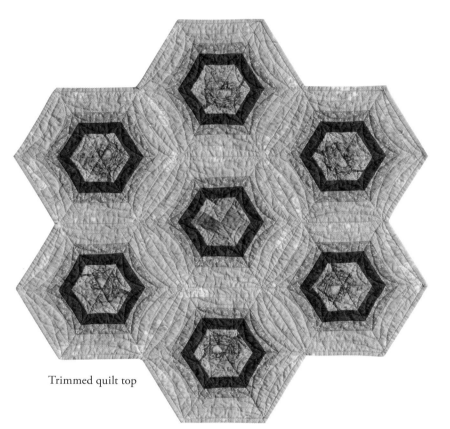

Trimmed quilt top

Binding quilts with inside and 60° corners requires a different process than binding 90° corners. Hexagon designs can be handled in a couple of different ways. The easiest way is to cut through the last round of hexagon pieces to create a straight edge. This often causes you to cut through a block, such as Grandmother's Flower Garden or Pinwheel; so you will need to decide how much work you want to put into the edge finish. If you want to retain the shapes, you can face the edge, fold in the seam allowances and do a knife-edge, or do an actual binding.

## Facing

A facing is a nice finish for irregular edges. If you do not want to cut through the blocks or pieces to get a straight edge, but you also do not want to bind every little hexagon, a facing might be the answer. A facing is also a clean finish on a quilt for which a binding would add bulk or a stripe that you do not desire. The final border is the actual edge of the quilt. This is not a durable finish, so take that into account if the quilt is going to be used on a bed or as a throw. Also take into consideration the color of the facing, as you will see the very edge of it at the seam on the edge of the quilt.

If the quilt is small, it is easiest to use a piece of fabric that is the size of the quilt, cutting away the interior of the fabric. This creates a piece of facing without any seams. It does take quite a bit of fabric, but if your quilt is an irregular shape, this is much easier than trying to join strips at odd angles at each corner. It also eliminates bulky seams.

When removing the center of the fabric, leave enough so that the facing is wide enough to extend beyond the deepest point of the edge plus 1″–2″.

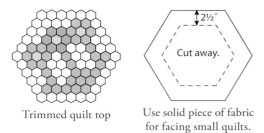

Trimmed quilt top

Use solid piece of fabric for facing small quilts.

If you are facing a larger quilt and do not want to waste so much fabric, make the facing from strips sewn together to accommodate your measurements. Cut the facing at least 2½″ wide. Cut the strips for the top and bottom of the quilt the width measurement. Cut the side strips the length of the quilt minus the top and bottom widths, plus 1″ for seam allowances. Once all 4 pieces are joined, press the seam allowances open. The corners will be cleaned up when you hand sew at the end.

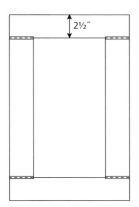

Sewing strips together for facing larger quilts

Before adding the facing, carefully trim the edges of the quilt exactly along each side of each shape. To sew the facing onto the quilt, position it on the right side of the quilt top, right sides together. Pin or baste to hold in place. You will be sewing from the backside, where you can see and guide along the edge. You might want to add dots ¼″ in along the seam at each pivot point for accuracy.

Begin stitching. As you approach each pivot point, shorten the stitches to add strength to the corners when the facing is turned. Stitch around the entire quilt.

Trim the seam allowances to ⅛″, making a clip at each inside point and trimming away most of the excess seam allowance on the outside points. This will give you a sharper point by eliminating the bulk and will allow the batting to form a miter inside the turned edge.

Turn the facing to the back, carefully pushing out the outside corners. Using a point turner to gently create the points is very helpful. Take your time and work carefully. This is not a quick process.

Turning point with point turner

As you turn the points, pin in place. Every once in a while, go to the ironing board and press the edge flat. Once all of the edges are turned, turn under the raw edge to establish a straight and even measurement from the inside points; hand stitch the folded edge in place.

Finished edge—front and back

# Knife-Edge

Another method to finish irregular edges is to turn in the edges of both the back and front, and whipstitch the edge. The batting needs to be trimmed to the seamline. Turn the top edge over the trimmed batting edge, and baste. Turn the backing in to match the folded edge of the top. You may also need to baste or press this edge to make it easier to stitch. Hand stitch with matching thread, using tiny overcast stitches.

Close-up of knife-edge finish

# Binding

If you have trimmed the sides of a hexagon quilt to straight edges, you may still encounter 60° corners. These are handled in the same manner as a square corner, but the turn is not a true miter. The process is the same but with a small adjustment.

If you are binding many inside and outside corners, be patient. There is a lot of turning and mitering involved.

Start the process by sewing a line of stitching, just a thread narrower than your seam allowance, around all the edges of the quilt. Make a small clip straight from the edge to the inside point, stopping just shy of the stitching. This will allow you to straighten the edge as you apply the binding.

Clipping inside corners

You will find that binding a complex edge like this is easier with narrow binding. We cut our bias strips ⅞″ wide, using a single thickness. This gives a ³⁄₁₆″ finished binding.

*Note* ❦ We use a single-thickness binding, as a double-fold binding is a bit bulky and stiff to work with. It is also very difficult to work with a double-fold binding when you want to create an edge this small. We suggest you make a couple of samples before beginning, as binding this type of edge is a very labor-intensive process, and you want to really like it in the end.

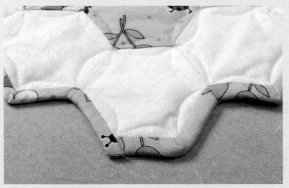

Side-by-side bindings—double-fold (*right*) and single-fold (*left*)

Start sewing the binding onto the edge. Be sure to leave about 8″–10″ at the beginning and start the sewing on an outside straight edge, if possible. Sew toward the first inside point and stop with your needle in the down position, using a seam allowance slightly wider than ⅛″.

Stop right at intersection.

Turn quilt to create straight edge.

With the needle still in the fabric, lift the presser foot and pull the edge straight behind the needle so that you create a straight edge. If you have a knee lift for your presser foot, this is a perfect place to use it. The clip that you made will allow the edge to straighten. Continue sewing. Notice that there is no miter here and that the binding is standing straight up. The miter will be formed when you hand stitch the binding into place.

Once you get to the outside corner, stop stitching at the seamline, turn the quilt, and backstitch off the edge, making sure you stay at the same angle as the raw edge on the right. You will not be stitching straight but at the 60° angle. Pull the quilt away from the needle and fold the binding up. Fold the binding over itself at the corner and align the raw edge of the binding and the edge of the quilt. This is exactly how you miter a square corner—but unlike a square corner, where all the edges align with each other, this time the binding will not align with the top edge of the quilt.

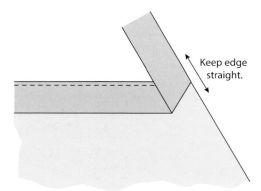

Turning 60° corner

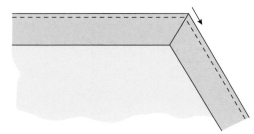

Turning 60° corner

Once you have been around all sides of the quilt, join the ends using either of the methods covered earlier, or your method of choice. Trim all the layers if necessary to keep the seam allowance exactly the same width. Turn the binding to the back, fold over the seam allowance, and align the folded edge with the seam. Hand stitch, using either a blind stitch (page 115) or a ladder stitch (page 116).

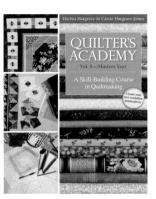

**Harriet Hargrave** has been in the quilt world for decades, changing how we quilt—by machine—with her best-selling book *Heirloom Machine Quilting*. She went on to write *Mastering Machine Appliqué*, *From Fiber to Fabric*, *The Art of Classic Quiltmaking* with Sharyn Craig, and most recently the Quilters Academy series that had her daughter Carrie Jones as a coauthor.

After owning her quilt store Harriet's Treadle Arts for 36 years and traveling for 32 years teaching around the world, the decision was made to retire and live out her dream of going back to the farm. She bought a beautiful 40-acre farm in central Missouri. Harriet now has fulfilled her dream of owning horses and has four that take a lot of her time and energy. Reestablishing the gardens is her other goal, keeping retirement exciting and challenging. Quilting has taken a back seat to horses, but teaching is still her passion and when asked, she is more than happy to share her knowledge with today's quilters.

**Carrie Jones**, her husband, and her son have joined Carrie's mom, Harriet, on the farm and in the adventure of country life. She is a stay-at-home mom and keeps their website going, along with a small store on the farm, Farm Stand Quilt Shop. All the quilts in the book were pieced and quilted by Harriet and Carrie. They truly believe that if you are going to teach it, you had better be able to make it!